The Art & Science of
Fly Fishing

The Art & Science of Fly Fishing

by H. LENOX H. DICK
drawings by Alan Pratt

THE CITADEL PRESS   SECAUCUS, N.J.

First paperbound printing, 1977
Copyright © 1966, 1972 by H. Lenox H. Dick
All rights reserved
Published by Citadel Press
A division of Lyle Stuart, Inc.
120 Enterprise Ave., Secaucus, N.J. 07094
Published by arrangement with Winchester Press, New York
Manufactured in the United States of America
ISBN 0-8065-0588-5

ACKNOWLEDGEMENTS

I MET SPENCER BIDDLE in Portland, Oregon in 1941 when I became engaged to his daughter. My family had informed me back in Philadelphia that Mr. Biddle liked to fish and did a great deal of it. Naturally, as a fisherman, I preferred a fisherman father-in-law to a non-fisherman, but I did not bother to find out just how good a fisherman he was.

I was a magnificent fisherman, having fished the Brodhead, the Tobyhanna, and other great Pennsylvania streams where two fish per trip was quite a feat for me. I had also surprised my guide by catching land-locked salmon on the Sardehunk River in Maine, (my "guide", who was all of seventeen years old, had never seen this done before) and I did not mention that the fish measured seven to twelve inches in length. Furthermore, I had read Halford and Skues; my copy of Hewitt's *Handbook of Fly Fishing* had been dunked in the water many times, and I knew most of Ray Bergman's books by heart.

The day after my arrival in Portland Mr. Biddle invited me to go fishing with him on a nearby river. He loaned me a beautiful rod, a rather mangy-looking pair of boots, and gave me the necessary flies. After rigging up at the stream I stood respectfully to one side so I could watch him fish.

Mr. Biddle walked out into the water a few feet, stripped from his reel a great deal of line which he coiled in his hand, and then, with about two false casts, he shot seventy feet of line across the pool. As the fly fluttered to the water my eyes must have stood out like a lobster's. Never had I seen anybody cast like that. I was in the presence of the mighty!

The stream was about four times larger than any I had seen in the East. I slunk around the bend looking for a likely place to fish. Finally I came to a spot where a log in the stream produced a small riffle. After my usual six or seven false casts, my fly landed on the log. To release the fly I gave the line a twitch and the rod tip broke under the strain.

I waded out and removed the fly. Then I sat down on a large rock with my head in my hands. What to do? Should I thumb a ride back to Philadelphia or stay and face the music? I decided to stay. Quickly I unravelled some threads from my handkerchief and carefully repaired the tip.

Starting to fish again, I soon met Mr. Biddle and, silently, handed him the rod. He looked at it and smiled.

"That's a dandy job of wrapping. I never would have thought of using threads from my handkerchief to wrap a rod tip." Then he added, "I knew that tip was weak. I was going to send it back to Powell this week."

Two beautiful steelhead glistened on the bank nearby and, though they were small late summer fish weighing three or four pounds, they were the most beautiful fish I had ever seen.

My next trip with Mr. B involved fly fishing from a boat. We were accompanied by Charlie Miller, one of the Northwest's great fly fishermen. (Clark Van Fleet devotes quite a bit of space in his fine book, *Steelhead To A Fly*, to Mr. Miller's fishing skills.) Mr. Biddle rowed, Mr. Miller fished from the stern, and I was casting from the bow. The river was slow; we were fishing for cutthroat.

"Lenox! You can't catch fish in trees!" Mr. Biddle would say to me with a smile. I didn't know what he meant. Suddenly Mr. Miller put down his rod, turned to Mr. Biddle and said, "Spencer! ————!! ———! ————! Why don't you teach your son-in-law to fish!"

Devastated, I put my rod down, picked up the oars and rowed for the rest of the day. From this time on I became a disciple of Mr. Biddle's and he became my teacher.

As I look back over my 20-year association with Mr. Biddle I have often wondered what did he precisely teach me and I have trouble. Then I realize why. This man was so modest and he taught me in such a manner that I felt I had discovered these things for myself. The one concrete fact I know I learned was the unity of fly fishing, dry fly, wet fly and nymph fishing are one and the same.

Knowledge is based on the discoveries of our predecessors. In writing this book I utilized the teaching of Spencer Biddle, coupled with a review of the fishing literature, going back to the works of Halford in the '90s and continuing up through Skues, Hewitt, La Branch, Tavner . . . until the present time.

I wish to express my appreciation to my wife for her patience and assistance during the course of writing this book.

The illustrator, Alan Pratt, is a master fly fisherman with the unique ability to read water and express it in his illustrations. Fortune smiled on this book when he consented to do the illustrations.

I would especially like to single-out Pete Hidy, author of Sports Illustrated's book on wet fly fishing. It was his initial encouragement that gave me the impetus to start to write. During the course of my writing Pete presented me with many valuable suggestions.

Fred Lock, of the Oregon State Game Commission and Stanley Jewett of the U.S. Fish and Wildlife Service rewrote the Chapter on Entomology.

Wayne Busek, Dan Bailey and Dr. Nat Wison gave me valuable assistance with nymph patterns.

Finally, I wish to express my appreciation to all the members of the Fly Fishers Club of Oregon who, over the years, have given so freely of their lore and experiences.

Spencer Biddle

To Spencer Biddle

Contents

Part III Salmon, Steelhead, & Others

Introduction

The *art* of fly-fishing is the skill and grace with which the angler casts his fly. The *science* of fly-fishing uses the knowledge of where fish are, how they feed, and how properly to present a fly. If the science of fly-fishing is neglected, trout are not caught regularly. This science may seem complex but can be reduced to the ability to read water and to achieve proper fly presentation.

There is no single way of fishing each of the various types of flies. A streamer can be fished as a dry fly; a nymph as a streamer. Nature presents food to fish in all these manners. We must constantly imagine how she would do it at a given time, place, and season.

The drawings and photographs that accompany this text place the reader at streamside. They teach him to read water, locate the trout, and then properly present his fly. Other important facts of fly fishing are also discussed.

A trout hooked on a small fly and played on a light, whippy fly rod brings out and magnifies every action. The thrill of landing a trout with a fly has a certain zest that cannot be duplicated by the same action with bait.

A fish caught on a fly may be returned to the stream to live, while one caught on bait usually dies due to having swallowed the barbed hook. Civilization has gravely reduced the fish population, especially species like trout which require cold, clear water. If we are to preserve stream fishing for future generations, we must fish for fun and not for food.

The Art & Science of
Fly Fishing

PART I
The Fundamentals

CHAPTER ONE

Basic Tackle

ONE OF THE MOST enjoyable experiences in fly-fishing is the ability to cast a fly consistently with ease for a satisfactory distance. Only balanced equipment will cast a fly properly. I urge you to heed the advice given in the following paragraph.

BASIC FLY ROD

The graph on the next page represents a composite of favorite rods, mine and Spencer Biddle's, for average trout fishing. This rod has a parabolic action, or a smooth bend from the butt to the tip when a 2-ounce weight is hung on the tip.

Up until recently, it was difficult for a beginner to obtain a properly balanced fly rod and line. In the past fifteen years fly-fishing has become so popular that specialized shops have appeared in just about every locale where there is trout fishing. Most shops have mail order catalogs in which they usually list a basic balanced outfit consisting of a 3½–4-ounce, 8- or 8½-foot fly rod with a double-tapered floating line and inexpensive single-action fly reel. These combinations have been selected by experts and perform well. Some stores list these in various price ranges. The inexpensive basic outfit will serve the beginner quite well. As you become proficient, you may find that your individual style of casting will perform better with a slightly different rod action. As much as possible, try out other fishermen's rod-and-line combinations as you progress in your fishing experience.

Some fly-fishing stores list 6- or 7-foot rods as basic fly rods. These little rods do cast a short line well, but are poor performers in any degree of wind. The basic 3½–4-ounce, 8½-foot rod will cast a long line with ease, and has a pleasant action whether you are landing a 6-inch trout or a 12-pound salmon.

FLY REELS

Fly reels serve only to hold line and do not participate in the actual fly casting. There is only one reason for owning a moderately priced reel instead of an inexpensive one: big fish! Any fish much over 10 inches should be played from the reel. Truly big trout, 3 pounds or over, may make long runs. The bearings of a cheap reel may bind, and away goes the fish! Most of the basic outfits sold in fly shops provide a moderately priced reel. These reels will last for many years. Be sure to buy an extra spool on which to carry your other line..

FLY LINES

In the last twenty-five years fly lines have vastly improved. In fact, it is difficult to purchase a bad line in the better grades. As you became proficient in the science of fly-fishing, you will be able to pick out an inexpensive line that will do the job almost as well as an expensive one.

The fishing techniques in this book are predicated on the premise that the fly-fisherman will have both a floating or sinking line available at all times. I prefer a double-tapered line for 90 percent of all trout fishing.

After you have practiced with your new basic outfit for a period of time, borrow a line one size heavier than was fur-

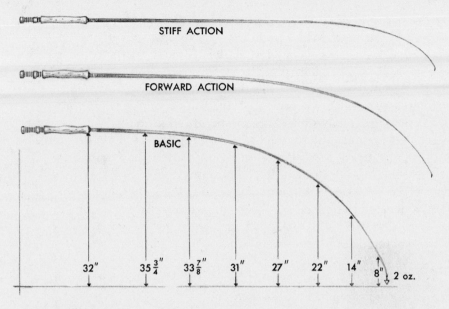

STIFF ACTION

FORWARD ACTION

BASIC

32" 35$\frac{3}{4}$" 33$\frac{7}{8}$" 31" 27" 22" 14" 8" 2 oz.

Fig. 1. Rod graph.

nished with the rod. You may find that your rod casts better.
The heavier weight of this line will usually make it cast better
into the wind than the lighter line.

LEADERS

A leader is a long strand of nylon or gut connecting the fly
to the line. In the past two decades nylon has replaced the old
silkworm gut leader. Nylon leaders are stronger and cast better;
furthermore, there is no need for soaking before use. The only
choice today is between a limp nylon and the German platyl
nylon.

Platyl is a stronger limp nylon material. It has less stretch
in it than the regular limp nylon. I prefer platyl leaders because
they are stronger. At the present time these are supplied only
as tapered, single-strand leaders. If the fisherman prefers a tied
leader, however, he may obtain this material in spools and tie
his own.

The best limp nylon leaders are tied leaders similar to the old gut ones. When properly tied, these cast a bit better than the single-strand, tapered leaders. I carry two sizes of leader, none shorter than nine feet. These are 2X and 4X. The 'X' designation refers to the diameter of the tip, 4X being quite fine. During the course of a day's fishing one frequently changes flies, gradually shortening the tip of the leader by 6 or 8 inches. This renders the tip too heavy and thick to properly present the fly without a great deal of disturbance in the water. It then becomes necessary either to tie on a new leader or lengthen the old. I carry with me spools of 2X, 4X, and 5X leader material in order to replace the tips of the leaders. At times, I may make a 4X leader into a 10- or 11-foot 5X leader by tying on extra 5X material. This long finely tapered leader is used with size #18 or #20 midge flies.

Before using a leader, stretch the kinks out, or else it will not lie straight on the water.

Enough about tackle. Fishing books, as a rule, spend too much time discussing equipment and not enough discussing fishing techniques.

CHAPTER TWO

Basic Fly Casting

IN FLY CASTING, the line is cast; in lure or bait casting, the lure is cast. It is possible to take a fly line and cast it with a non-bending broom handle purely by wrist action combined with the weight and balance of the line. The actual performance resembles hammering a nail into a vertical wall, with a pause at the top of the backward stroke, allowing the line to straighten out behind. This is followed by the forward stroke. The old method of teaching concentrated on wrist action with the elbow held against the side. Today the student is instructed to keep the wrist stiff and let the elbow and shoulder do the work. However, if using your wrist comes instinctively to you, then use it. The secret of fly casting lies in the tip of the rod, as indicated in Fig. 2. In the hands of an expert, fly casting ap-

Fig. 2.

Fig. 3. Expert casting.

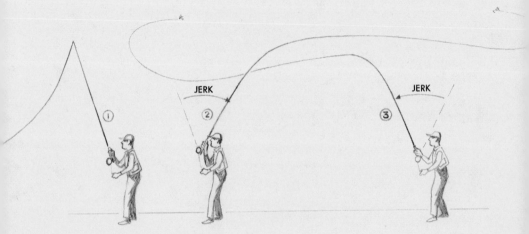

Fig. 4. Make the tip work.

pers as a smooth, graceful performance (Fig. 3), but if we break it down into its component parts, it becomes a jerky performance. If the novice will concentrate on smoothing out the jerky aspects he will be able to cast an acceptable line in fifteen minutes. The deliberate jerk makes the tip work—*that* is the secret. *Make the tip work* . . . Fig. 4!! First, strip 15 feet of line from the reel; it is a good idea to measure this. Hold the arm and hand in the position shown in the drawing with the rod at the 10 o'clock position. Don't worry about the wrist, elbow and shoulder; they will instinctively take care of themselves. Instead, *concentrate on the jerky action of the tip.* Bring the rod quickly back to the 1 o'clock position, allowing the line to fall to the ground in back of you. Look around; you will find the line is straight out in back. With the rod still in the 1 o'clock position, bring it forward smartly just like hammering the nail, and stop it again at 10 o'clock. If you forget that you are holding a fly rod and pretend you are hammering nails, *with a pause between the backward and forward stroke,* you will have the basic fundamentals of fly casting. Concentrate on making that tip work! Practice this simple maneuver for five minutes. Next, consciously turn your head as the line goes back and, before it strikes the ground, start the forward stroke. If the line cracks like a whip, you are starting the forward stroke too soon. Practice until your timing is right.

Lengthening the Line

Now that you have learned the fundamentals of casting, you must learn to bring in the line properly. This is accomplished by holding the line in the same hand as the rod and pulling the line in with the opposite hand. The excess line is caught and coiled in the pulling hand, Fig. 5.

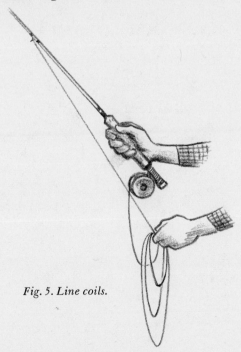

Fig. 5. Line coils.

To lengthen the cast, strip off line with the left hand and allow it to go back with a back cast or forward with a forward cast. This is referred to as false casting.

When I first fished with Spencer Biddle, he used to turn to me with a glint in his eye and say, "Brother, three false casts are all you are allowed. After that, the line falls in the water and *you fish*, no matter how bad a cast it may be! There are no fish in the trees on this stream."

There is a point where the length of the line balances the action of the rod, after which the line starts to drop down behind you. When this point is reached, borrow some of your wife's red nail polish and daub it on the line just where it comes through the top guide. This will make it easy for you to find the balance point the next time you cast. When this point is reached, if the angler desires to lengthen his cast, more line should be pulled from the reel and coiled in the left hand. Then, when the forward cast is reached, the line is allowed to shoot out . . . thereby lengthening the cast by many feet.

The expert angler, about to start his cast, strips from the reel the necessary amount of line that he thinks he will need for his entire cast, coils this in his left hand in loose coils (Fig. 5), makes two false casts and shoots the remainder of the line.

The Roll-Cast

The next basic cast the angler must learn is the roll cast (See Fig. 6). This allows the fisherman to cast his line while standing next to a high bank, under a tree, or wherever a back-cast is inadvisable. If your rod is too stiff you will not cast well. The basic rod will roll-cast with ease. However, the line must be balanced to the rod and it must be heavy enough. If your rod does not cast well, try a whippier or softer rod or else try a heavier line on your present rod.

Now, cast 15 feet of line in front of you and then carefully follow the illustration. Bring the rod back 2 feet with a straight

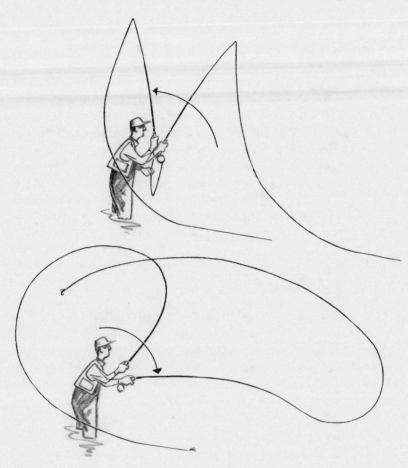

Fig. 6. Roll cast.

arm so that your hand and shoulder are back and opposite each other. Bring the arm and shoulder forward quickly and, at the same time, hammer that nail with your wrist. Lo! The line gracefully rolls out and you have made your first roll cast! With the proper rod and line, the roll-cast is a cinch!

When fishing, pick your line off the water with a roll cast before starting the next cast. This allows you to bring the fly in close, pick up 15 or 20 feet of line easily and decrease the amount of false casting necessary to shoot out the next cast.

Straight Cast with S Curves

A great deal of the time, the fisherman fishes upstream and allows his fly to drift down toward him in a natural manner.

In order to avoid drag it is necessary to cast upstream or down with many S curves in the line. An example of this is shown in Figs. 10 and 11, page 35

Cast exactly as you did while performing the basic straight cast. Instead of the usual follow-through to the 10 o'clock position, stop the rod abruptly at 11 o'clock. You will note that the line will fall with many S curves in it. The size of the S curves can be varied by the amount of followthrough utilized.

Curved Upstream Cast

You will frequently read in fishing literature about the curved upstream cast. This is a cast for the expert.

Face upstream on the left bank of the stream. Instead of holding your rod in a vertical position, hold it out from you at a 45-degree angle. Cast the fly exactly as you did with the regular fly cast we described previously. You have now performed a straight-side-arm cast. Now, cast again, but do not put sufficient power in the forward cast to straighten out the line! *Voila!* You have performed a curved upstream cast.

Most fishermen are capable of performing this cast only about half of the time. A straight quartering upstream cast with S curves in the line will do almost as well. Whenever this cast is mentioned, keep this fact in mind. Both of these casts are used to prevent drag.

Mending a Cast

That old devil "drag" will plague you all your fishing career. Many times a day when you make a cast, the current will take the belly out of your line and your fly will drag. This calls for

Fig. 7. Line mending.

putting another curve in your line without actually recasting the line. In order to do this, we "mend" the line.

Lower the tip of your rod close to the water. At the same time take a little slack line from the reel and hold it in your left hand. Then with your rod tip make a partial side-roll-cast . . . up, over, and down . . . in the upstream direction, allowing at the same time the slack line to shoot out of your left hand. This must be done with just enough power to pick up the part of your line that is curved downstream, but not enough to disturb the fly. See Fig. 7. Another way to describe this cast is a side-arm-roll cast. This is a most valuable cast and can be used anytime there is drag.

There are many other casts used in fly fishing . . . so many, in fact, that when I read books on fly casting I become hopelessly confused. They are all variations of the casts I have described. When you have become proficient in their use you will instinctively learn many others.

You will probably want to learn the double-haul cast in the future. This technique will add a third more distance to your cast. However, Spencer Biddle, the greatest practical fly-fisherman I ever watched, never consciously used the double-haul.

As there are fishermen who spend most of their time tying flies, there are fishermen who emphasize fly casting to the detriment of the rest of their fishing prowess.

CHAPTER THREE

Fly Presentation

IN THIS BOOK we fish together. You will be at my elbow or close by throughout. I want you to have the feeling and mood of actual participation. Put on your waders, gather up your gear, and we will go to a stream.

I would like to suggest that you always wear a fishing vest with a built-in life preserver. Once you have seen a careless fisherman floating face down in a river you will learn to be extremely cautious, especially in big rivers. Many of the waters we will fish together in this book will fall into that category. The pool you and I will fish today is in a relatively small river, but it can be boated even at this stage, and fishermen have drowned during high water.

Look over Plate 4, page 89, carefully so that you have a good mental picture. Now, look at the line drawing, Fig. 20, page 88, and find the various common landmarks. Remember, the pictures in this book are taken so that you are looking upstream and the water is flowing toward you.

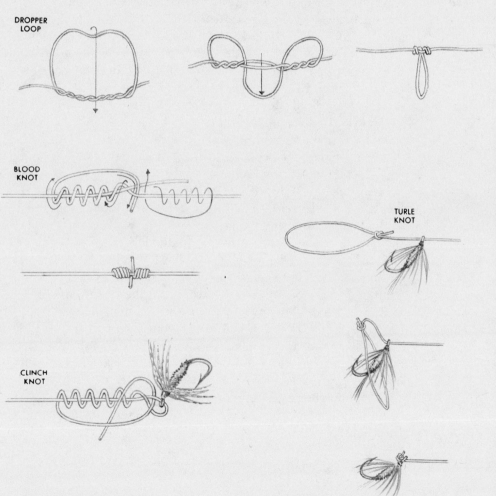

Fig. 8. Knots.

Now, rig up your rod with your sinking or wet fly line. Tie on a 9½-foot 2X leader and a number 10 Bucktail Coachman. Please note Fig. 8 for instruction in tying various knots. The leader is heavier than you will usually use, but it will be easier to cast for your initial lesson in fly presentation.

Walk up to the pool and stand at fishing position 2; Plate 4, Fig. 20. Cast 30 feet of line straight out in front of you; watch carefully what happens to your fly and line as it swings downstream below you. A downstream belly will form in the line and the fly will be quickly dragged around, away from you. The fly will cover very little water. A cast straight out from the fisherman is little used in stream fly fishing. Repeat this cast and watch what happens to the fly and leader. The chances are that your fly floated on the surface until it had swung well below you. By that time the line had sunk and the fly had been pulled under the surface. If you had actually been fishing, your fly would have first been a floating but dragging dry fly and then, as the line swung around and the fly sank, it would have been a sunken wet fly with a tight line and drag. (Dry and wet flies are tied differently but they can be used interchangeably. If this seems confusing, don't worry . . . as we fish together in the chapters to come, this will gradually clear up.)

You have seen what happens to the fly and line when cast straight out; now, to learn to properly present your fly! This chapter and the one on reading water are the two most important in the book. Master these and you will have mastered the fundamentals of fly-fishing. Present your fly properly, in the right place and any of a dozen flies will catch fish for you. Surprisingly, a majority of fly fishermen do not know the rudiments of fly presentation. Yet, to consistently catch fish you should know the basic techniques of presentation. Broken down into fundamentals, these are simple techniques with numerous variations.

Quartering Down and Across (Wet Fly)

Go back to where you were standing before, but instead of casting directly across the current, turn slightly and cast the

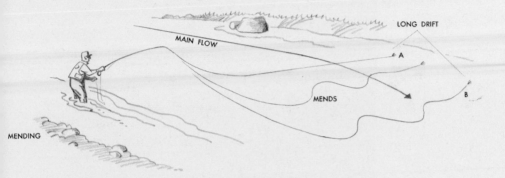

Fig. 9. Quartering downstream cast with mends

line at a 45-degree angle downstream (Fig. 9). Instead of immediately casting 30 feet of line, cast only 15 feet and allow the
line to swing down before you. Notice the difference. A belly
did not form in your line as soon as it did with the straight
cast, and your fly stayed out farther in the current for a longer
time.

Now the fly is below you. Bring it back with little twitches
or jerks. You have now performed a quartering downstream
cast—the commonest cast used in presenting a wet fly. It can
also be used for streamer flies, nymph flies, nymphs, and dry
flies. Next time, cast about 20 feet and repeat the process. The
next . . . cast 30 feet, etc. Why not cast 30 to 50 feet at the
start? One of the grave errors in fly presentation is over-fishing
the water or casting too long a line and thereby casting a line
over a fish and putting him down before you have a chance to
catch him.

Practice that cast for about five minutes. Remember, start
fishing close to you and then gradually work your fly out. Who
knows, there may be fish in that water and you might catch one.

You have practiced long enough. You are committing a
grave error by picking your line up off the water too soon,
because you were not satisfied with the cast. This causes a
slurping effect and, again, will scare away the fish. Whenever
your fly and line strike the water . . . leave them . . . and *don't*

pick them up, no matter how bad the cast, until they swing downstream from you. It is surprising how many fish I've caught with casts I did not like but fished out anyway.

You are now ready for a variation in the quartering downstream presentation. Cast your fly exactly as before, but when your fly lands at A allow it to drift to B. At this point strip more line from the reel, thereby causing the line to slow down and stay in the middle of the current for a while longer. When the fly is below you, allow it to stop for at least a minute. Fish often strike at this point. They follow the fly until it finishes its swing and then will take it as it stops. At times they pause before taking it. If you are overly anxious, you will miss the strike. Now bring the fly back with little twitches.

A final variation of the quartering downstream technique is as follows: Cast your fly downstream at a 45-degree angle. Allow it to drift a foot or two and then put a mend in your line (Fig. 9). Notice that the fly drifts downstream without drag. Each time it appears that the fly may drag, throw another mend in your line. This technique is used whenever drag is not wanted, such as when presenting a dry fly or a wet fly with a natural drift.

Quartering Upstream (Dry Fly)

Change your line from the sinking to the floating one. Cast your fly, quartering upstream, with a few S curves in the line as shown in Fig. 10. This is the usual manner of fishing a dry fly. It is easier to make a fly float without drag when fishing upstream. An added advantage is that the sounds of your wading are carried away from the fish. As the fly floats downstream, retrieve some line (depending on the speed of the water); too much slack line will cause you to miss the fish if it rises for the fly. When the fly ceases its natural float, it should be allowed to swing well below before you quietly retrieve the line and recast. This is to prevent disturbing any fish that may be near you.

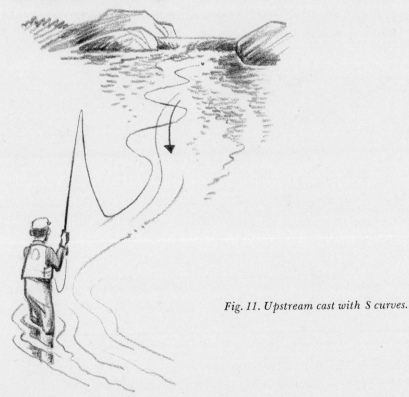

Fig. 10. Quartering upstream cast with big curve

The technique of the upstream quartering cast with a slack line may be used to fish a sunken wet fly or nymph. When cast upstream, the fly sinks deeper than it would with the quartering downstream method because it does not have the pull of the line to drag it up to the surface.

Some experts are able to cast a big upstream curve in their lines instead of the S curves we use. When this method is referred to in the future, remember that the S curves are simpler and will do as well.

Fig. 11. Upstream cast with S curves.

Directly Upstream (Dry Fly)

The fly is cast directly upstream. It will drift straight toward you, either on the surface or at varying depths beneath the surface. The line must be retrieved rapidly without disturbing the fly, so that you can successfully strike the fish. This technique is particularly effective when fishing close to the bank of a stream (Fig. 11). Occasionally, it may be used in wet fly fishing.

Directly Downstream (Dry or Wet Fly)

This cast is used primarily for the dry fly. However, it is also used to present a nymph or wet fly with a natural float. The fisherman casts the fly in such a manner that large S curves are placed in the line. The straightening-out of these S curves allows the fly to float naturally until the line is straight. A further float may be obtained by stripping line from the reel and wagging the rod tip to produce more S curves. This technique is particularly applicable to fishing downstream under trees and other obstructions. See Fig. 12.

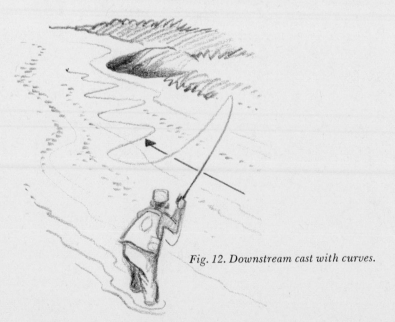

Fig. 12. Downstream cast with curves.

Variations in these four techniques will be brought out and amplified in the chapter on stream tactics. When talking to fishing experts keep in mind that there are only four basic techniques . . . then you will be able to break down their complicated discussions into one of these. Your own variations of these techniques will come almost instinctivey as you progress in fishing.

CHAPTER FOUR

Reading Water

YOU HAVE SPENT enough time practicing casting. For the next two days we will drive around to various rivers and we will practice reading water together. Obviously, the pictures used to illustrate this book were taken in different regions. They represent portions of streams in Oregon, Washington and British Columbia. However unfamiliar the terrain may appear, the basic water characteristics may be found in any stream in North America.

Fish are where you find them, sometimes where you least expect them. An inexperienced angler may read water well on one stream and be completely lost on another only a few miles away. An example: Steelhead that are inclined to strike a fly are more often found on the Rogue River at the tail-end of pools in the region of the break, whereas in Northern Oregon and Washington streams they seem to lie more toward the head of the pool. In a few trout streams the fish seem to feed avidly in the boils, while in others I am never successful in raising a fish in boils.

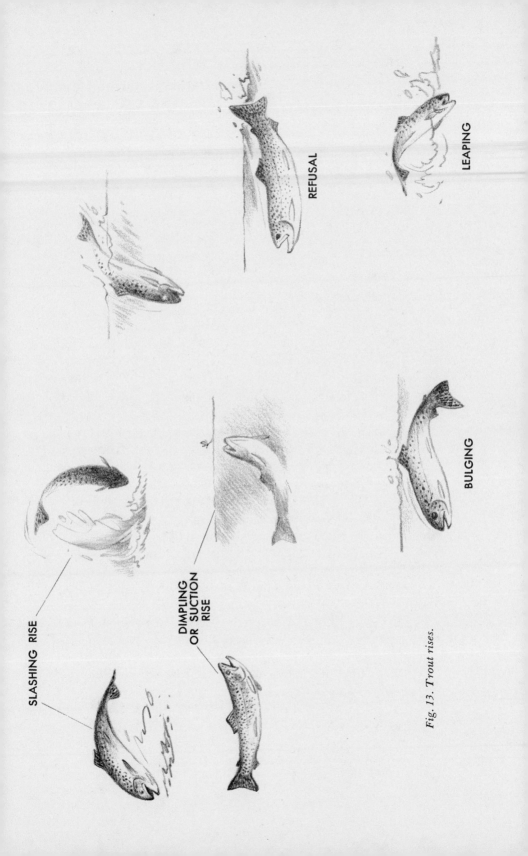

REFUSAL

LEAPING

SLASHING RISE

DIMPLING OR SUCTION RISE

BULGING

Fig. 13. Trout rises.

However, an angler with a good basic knowledge of reading water can come to a new stream and know immediately where many good fish are located. This fundamental knowledge will prevent wasting time fishing barren water. Reading water is considered by some to be a sixth sense. These individuals write knowingly of this sense. This is nonsense. It is simply a matter of experience.

On bright days wear polaroid glasses. They will allow you to see deep in the water. Keep your eyes open for feeding fish, both on the top and on the bottom. Note the various trout rises illustrated in Fig. 13. You will very quickly learn to recognize this phenomenon. A fish may appear to be standing on his head (tailing) when he is feeding on the bottom. Feeding on nymphs, he may swirl around in the middle layers or bulge his back (bulging rises) when taking them near the surface. Then, there are the round rings (suction rises) on the surface, produced deliberately by trout feeding on floating mayflies. Splashing or slashing rises are caused by trout coming all the way out of the water, sometimes making a complete arc, and taking the fly on the way into the water. The refusal rise is the most frustrating. A trout will be seen coming up for a dry fly and then deliberately turn and head back down just before he should have taken the fly. Change to a smaller fly and he usually will take it.

Many times it is difficult to tell the difference between a suction rise on the surface and a bulging rise from a trout feeding close to the surface. How many times have I fished a dry fly on top when I should have used a wet fly just under the surface.

Study streams at all water levels, especially during low, clear water when hidden ledges and pockets can be clearly seen. Some anglers draw maps of the streams on which they mark the topography and prevalent conditions. Most of us commit these facts to memory.

Fishing for any species of trout or salmon is seldom very good when water is rising. This is true for a rise due to rain, melting snow, or water suddenly released from a dam. Fishing is usually excellent when water is falling. I have had good fishing on streams in flood as long as the water was falling.

Fish occupy three types of water: resting or holding water, feeding water, and passage water. Fish occupy passage water only transiently while traveling on migration or going to and from holding water. In the case of trout, holding and feeding water are frequently one and the same thing. Fish, like humans, must seek out dining rooms to obtain their food. Fish dining rooms are located where converging currents bring food.

A stream may be broken into component parts, no matter what its size.

A. Riffles and rapids
B. Obvious pools (oval, curved and cut-bank)
    1. Head of pool
    2. Middle
    3. Tail, break and slick
C. Deflectors
D. Straight section of stream (a reach)
    1. Undercut banks
    2. Sloping or shelving banks
E. Rocks
F. Large back-eddies
G. Boils
H. Whirlpools

In all of the plates the water is flowing toward you.

Riffles and Rapids

Any discussion of water reading should first clearly define a riffle. Plate 5 shows a typical large, shallow riffle; likewise the right side of the isand, Plate 14. A riffle is a fast-moving portion of a stream with many waves. These waves are formed by boulders in the bottom of the stream. Many times rocks protrude above the surface of the water. A riffle may be likened to a slow rapid. Many riffles containing fish are fast enough to be considered rapids as seen in Plates 6 and 7 and Fig. 22. I am

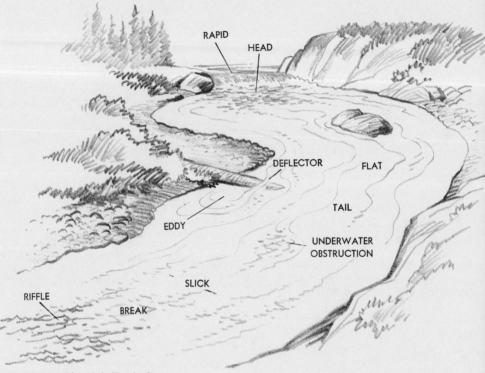

Fig. 13A. Typical water.

constantly amazed to find fish feeding in such water. The secret lies in the ability of the fish to seek out and lie in slow water behind rocks and, less often, in front of rocks. Some riffles lead into pools (Plate 2, Fig. 18), and some out (Plate 3, Fig. 19). Whether they lead in or out, those that are not too fast may contain trout.

Pools

Typical pools, shown in Plates 2, 3 and 4, Figs. 18, 19 and 20, have a riffle or a rapid at the head. Some even have water-falls. As the riffle or rapid flows into the pool the current gradually slows. The center of the pool contains slow, deep water. The tail-end, or final third, usually has a shelving bottom that gradually shallows until it forms a lip or break. This can be likened to slowly pouring water out of a cup. Where the water flows over the rim of the cup is the break and immediately below this is a short stretch of smooth, fast water–the slick–followed by the riffle, (Plate 3, Fig. 19). These are the component parts. Trout have definite areas that they seek out at various times of the day and season.

Oval pools are scarce and, for the most part, are found on small streams, frequently made by men or beavers. Plate 1, Fig. 18, shows the upper two thirds of an oval pool in a remote, small stream in Canada. The usual pool in a trout stream or river is curved.

Now to locate the fish. The last third of the riffle, leading into a pool, is a favorite feeding place. If the current is not too fast, the entire riffle may contain fish. If there are enough large rocks or boulders in a riffle, it may even be a resting area.

The constant movement of small stones and gravel in a riffle dislodges nymphs and other insect larvae, which the current brings down to the waiting fish. Nymphs live in riffles because of the relative increase in water oxygenation and abundance of their food. Trout seek out riffles during dusk in the summer months. In the spring they may be found feeding in these areas all day. On sunny days, early in the spring, when water is cold and murky, trout seek out slow and shallow riffles that they would never go near in the latter part of the season. The warmth of the sun on the water and the better visibility is a popular theory for this phenomenon.

As the riffle enters the pool, there will be noted a slow current at the side (Plate 1, Fig. 14; Plate 2, Fig. 18). Where the swift and slow currents come together, food collects, and there the fish are found. This is one of the most likely places to find big, feeding fish. The water is usually deep enough for large fish to sink down, hide, and watch the surface for insects. The fisherman who looks carefully will note that the fast and slow water will frequently form a point similar to the apex of a tri-

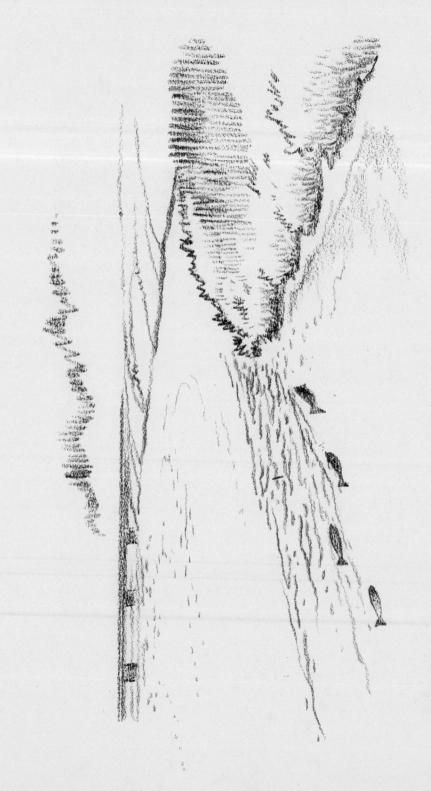

Fig. 14. Coffin corner.

Plate 1.

angle just as the riffle breaks in the pool (Plate 1, Fig. 14; Plate 2, Fig. 18 at H). Mr. Biddle used to refer to this as "coffin corner." Here, if it is deep enough, there is a tremendous collection of food, and that is where the big ones frequently lie.

Many pools contain whirlpools and big boils, and in some streams the fish feed avidly in the boils but seldom in whirlpools.

The deep, middle portion of a pool is seldom productive for fly fishermen (Plate 3, Fig. 19). Here, fish rest or hold, usually at the bottom. Occasionally, during a big hatch of caddis or stonefly, big fish come from the bottom and deliberately take a fly. Unless this rare phenomenon is occurring, don't bother with this section of the pool.

At the tail-end of the pool, in the region of the break, is a favorite spot for steelhead or salmon to lie (Plate 3, Fig. 19). This is also the location of many spawning beds and spawned-out fish. If there are rocks, boulders, or other obstructions, trout also like to lie, rest, and feed here. The corners of these areas are favorite locations for trout, providing it is deep enough and there is current.

Cut-Bank Pools

The inside curve of a cut-bank pool is usually shallow and gradually becomes deeper until it becomes a sheer bank or cut-bank (Plate 4, Fig. 20). This sheer bank is formed by water erosion. Everything written about curved pools holds for cut-bank pools with the exception that fish tend to lie and feed in against the cut-bank the entire length of the pool. This is particularly true of anadromous fish (fish that go to sea when 6-8 inches long and return as adults; see Chapter 12.)

Deflectors

Deflectors produce some of the best fishing water in a stream. An example is the log that extends out from the bank (Plate 3, Fig. 19). Fish will rest behind this log and occasionally in front,

Fig. 14A. Typical trout water.

enjoying the shade, concealment, and reduced current. At the tip of the farthest log there will be noted a definite change in the main current. This illustrates the principle of a joining of fast and slow current. Here, fish may be both resting and feeding. The angler must be alert for the deflector effect. At times, deflectors will be noted to consist of rocks, stumps, or branches which jut out into a stream (Plate 11). Very large deflectors frequently produce curved pools, curved riffles, and eddies.

Back Eddies

Back eddies, found in all types of pools, are an area of reverse current produced by a fast main current striking the bank at such an angle as to deflect it backward (Plate 3, Fig. 19). They are ideal collecting areas for food, and most trout find them excellent dinner tables. Unfortunately, back eddies, like whirlpools and boils, do not photograph well; they must be seen under actual stream conditions to be appreciated.

Shaded Areas

Trout are particularly aware of shaded areas in a stream (Plates 11 and 12, Fig. 25) as places to hide from birds of prey and as a ready source of insects dropping from the branches and overhanging grass. They will inhabit much shallower water where there is shade. This rule applies primarily to resident trout and not as much to sea-run fish. During the periods of big fly hatches, they frequently seem to wait under the shade from branches of trees for the various flies to fall off into the water.

Undercut Banks

Many streams are deep and straight, with undercut banks (Plate 10, Fig. 24). The water next to the bank may be as deep as 6 feet and extend in under the bank 6-12 inches. There is usually grass hanging over the water. However, the bank of a stream may actually be a moss bed (Plate 13, Fig. 26) extending into the stream, as is so typical of Silver Creek in Idaho. Trout lie under these banks, resting and feeding. They will feed on insects within inches of their resting place, or they may swim out and feed in the main current.

Ledges

Sea-run fish and trout love to lie near sunken ledges. Unfortunately, these ledges are frequently not visible to the angler on the first visits to the stream. The resident angler has a distinct advantage over the visitor in that he can examine the terrain during low water.

Tributaries

On any stream, be on the lookout for smaller streams flowing into the mainstream. If there is sufficient flow, fish are found lying above and below the mouth of the stream. A stream of sufficient size to constitute a spawning stream should be examined carefully by the angler for sea-run fish at its mouth. These fish collect in bunches at such locations in preparation for their final dash to the spawning bed.

At times of high, muddy water these small feeder streams may be the only place that the fisherman can fish his fly. They will form areas of clear water in the muddy water of the main stream.

Islands

Many large streams have islands scattered along their courses. The more difficult the island is to reach, the better is the fishing. John Q. Public does not like to walk or wade in difficult places. Remember, trying to wade to an island is a dandy way to drown. Wear an adequate life preserver or don't fish islands. Plate 14, Fig. 27 illustrates a large island. There are large rocks on the left side just opposite the large tree. Behind these are some real hot spots. Observe carefully the water extending behind the island. The current from each side of the island gradually comes together and extends downstream at least 100 feet. In this location I have caught many of my biggest trout. This is a natural banquet hall.

Hidden Pools

Most of the time we read water from the top down. Plate 7 appears as a simple, flat piece of water. We look at the bottom first. Lo! There is a 75-foot-long pool about 6 feet in depth.

On some slow, meandering rivers, providing the water is clear, careful scrutiny of the bottom will soon reveal pools with typical deflectors, rocks, etc. With this knowledge, the angler presents his fly properly.

Brown trout occupy the same location as rainbow, but brown trout prefer slower-moving streams. Many brown trout streams require bottom reading.

I begin to sense a feeling of impatience. Do not despair. In the chapter on fishing techniques we will retrace our steps and fish all the water that I have described. My! The fish we'll catch!

CHAPTER FIVE

Entomology

HERE ARE THE water-bred insects fly fishermen need to know:

ORDER OF AQUATIC INSECTS

Common Name	*Latin Name*
Mayfly	Ephemeroptera
Caddis fly	Trichoptera
Stonefly	Plecoptera
True fly (Midge)	Diptera
Dragonfly	Odonata

Here are the land-bred insects fly fishermen should know:

ORDER OF TERRESTRIAL INSECTS

Common Name	*Latin Name*
Grasshopper	Orthoptera
Bee and ant	Hymenoptera
Beetle	Coleoptera
True fly	Diptera
Moth	Lepidoptera

A fly fisherman will have no great difficulty differentiating the three most important aquatic flies: mayfly, caddis fly, and stonefly. All three have two sets of wings. Most mayflies have only a rudimentary second pair. While at rest the mayfly holds its wings in a vertical position.

Identifying either the caddis fly or the stonefly is not difficult. The caddis, when at rest, holds its wings over its body like a peaked roof. The stonefly's wings are folded flat over the body.

STONEFLY AND NYMPH   FLY AND NYMPH

MIDGE

CADDIS AND CASED LARVA

CADDIS AND STONEFLY AT REST

Fig. 15. Natural flies and nymphs.

Mayflies

The mayfly deserves first attention. While true flies, mostly tiny, inconspicuous kinds, are of primary importance as trout food, the mayfly is most commonly noticed by anglers. This insect goes through four stages in its life cycle. The nymph hatches from the egg, transforms after attaining full growth to the dun, and finally reaches the spinner stage.

In the nymph stage, the insect is entirely aquatic. It undergoes several changes of skin before it reaches the final point and floats or swims to the surface to finally break out of its last nymphal skin to the dun. An erratic path may be followed when the mature nymph floats or swims upward; it may go up and down, somewhat like an elevator, before it finally floats on the surface.

As a nymph, the mayfly is an even more important source of food than as a floating fly. Trout spend most of their time foraging on the bottom for this kind of food. Larvae of tiny true flies, caddis flies, and the nymphs of mayflies make up the majority of this food. Stonefly nymphs comprise a smaller part of the food supply.

Mayfly nymphs are commonly found under and around rocks. The nymphs of the giant mayfly, commonly referred to in the adult stage as drakes, occupy areas of silt but not of compact sand or mud. Most mayfly nymphs, however, are found in rocky areas. Their color varies with the color of the stream bottom. The commonest colors are dark brown backs and brown, olive-green, or yellow bellies.

Some nymphs crawl from place to place, some swim part of the time, and others burrow in silt or loose sand.

For years I was confused about flat- and round-bodied mayfly nymphs. They both hatch into mayflies. Most flat-bodied nymphs live around or under rocks in relatively fast water and have the ability to crawl. Most round-bodied nymphs live in silt or slow-water situations; some of these can actually swim to new locations. The nymphal stage of mayflies may last in some cases for as long as two years, but most nymphs become adults in three to six months. They undergo several changes of skin before they emerge from the water.

Trout feeding on the bottom for nymphs, at times, appear to be standing on their heads (tailing) as they nudge around the rocks and gravel. When this condition exists, the fisherman should use a deeply sunk nymph fly or nymph. How many times have I fished over large swirls on the surface to no avail, only to realize that I was fishing over trout taking nymphs floating close to the surface. Under these conditions the dry fly is worthless. A nymph sunk one or two feet beneath the surface is more logical.

Shortly after the nymph arrives at the surface, the skin splits open and the first fly stage, or dun, struggles out to ride the discarded skin as a raft. Duns, at this stage, are very weak fliers. They are called duns because their wings have a smoky, dull appearance. The mayfly is most succulent and nutritious at this stage. Trout prefer this form and feed avidly, rising slowly and deliberately to suck in the fly. This produces characteristic suction rings on the water.

When they reach full growth, duns usually fly directly up into the air and land in bushes and trees, where they again shed their skin and transform to the final spinner stage. The angler can tell a dun hatch simply by watching these insects fly slowly up into the air. When the fly returns to the water, it is no longer a dun but a glistening spinner. Some refer to the mayfly egglaying process as "spinning her eggs," hence the term spinner.

Spinners and duns look very much alike to the untrained eye; however, there is usually a difference in color. The spinner's body and wings are brighter, the belly is lighter in color, and the dark markings on the back are sharper in contrast. When the dun sits on the water, half of the body is curled off of the surface. In contrast, in one group of mayflies the female spinner floats flat on the water, since she must extend her body full-length to utilize the current to help strip or spin the hundreds of eggs from her two egg sacs.

The spinner of other mayflies may drop her eggs in flight or even crawl under the surface and lay them on a submerged rock or stick. Before laying her eggs, the female spinner mates in the air with a male spinner, usually over land. Shortly after mating, the male dies, and his body usually falls to the ground. The ripe female spinner then flies down, deposits some eggs, quickly rises, lands in another location, and repeats the process. Her time on the water is sometimes only momentary. Trout must rise quickly to catch the fly. This accounts for the slashing rises, with the fish frequently coming entirely out of the water.

Finally, the female spinner falls to the surface, often with her wings outstretched. Anglers refer to such a female as a spent-wing spinner. Spent-wing dry flies, with wings tied in a horizontal position, represent this fly. The spent-wing spinner contains little nutrition, though trout may feed widely on them at times.

Big hatches of mayflies usually do not occur until the water temperature reaches about 52°. However, I have seen good hatches appear with snow falling and the water temperature in the 40's. In my experience these hatches consist of small mayflies. In the Pacific Northwest they appear at any time during the winter months. I have never seen them, though, when there was ice in the water.

Caddis Flies (Sedges)

The caddis fly and its larva is just as important or more important on some streams than the mayfly. It varies in size from tiny to giant flies 2 inches in wing span. The caddis larva is best described as a round grub or creeper in a case. It may be pale yellow, white, or blue-green in color. Shortly after it hatches from the egg, the caddis immediately starts the construction of a suitable case or house. The type of case is typical of a specific group of these flies, and every member of that group will build a case of approximately the same material and pattern; thus, caddis worms of the same species are easily identified. Some employ gravel, some vegetable matter, and some a combination of both, binding them and cementing them together with a silken substance that the worm excretes. The cases are of various shapes, most often cylindrical or tapered. Some species live on the sides of rocks, behind screens of brush and aquatic plants that serve as nets to trap their food supply. Others drag their cases as they crawl over the bottom of the stream. The familiar "periwinkle," known to all fishermen, is one of the crawling variety. The case protects it from predatory stonefly and dragonfly nymphs. Trout eat the caddis worm, case and all, and have no difficulty expelling the empty cases.

When the caddis worm reaches maturity, it seals up the front end of its case, develops into the pupal stage, and acquires wing cases. It awakens from the period of dormancy, tears open the sealed end, and emerges, swathed in a thin membrane. The insect swims to the surface. With middle legs free of the sheath, the sheath is broken, and the winged caddis takes flight.

After arriving at the winged stage, the caddis fly does not change in structure, as does the mayfly, and is ready for mating and egg-laying at once.

I have seen caddis flies emerging only once. This was in the summer at late dusk. They apparently hatch out during the night. Probably all caddis flies consume water and perhaps other liquids with their sucking-type mouth parts. For this reason, the adult caddis, unlike the mayfly, may live for a matter of weeks. They often fly in swarms, usually close to the surface of the water. At sunset they may swarm over the tips of the trees, forming a dancing halo. They mate in mid-air in a fashion somewhat similar to mayflies.

The various species of caddis use different methods of egg laying. Some females skim along the surface, using the water film to strip eggs from their bodies. They appear to be fluttering along the water. In British Columbia these are known as "traveling sedges." Other kinds drop to the water's surface, rise up in the air, again and again, in a fashion similar to the mayfly spinner. Still other caddis flies dive to the surface from the air and swim down to lay their eggs under water. Some caddis flies crawl down on the sides of rocks, sticks, etc., and deposit their eggs.

Stonefly (Salmon Fly, Willow Fly)

The stonefly is to trout what filet mignon is to man. This was recognized by Sir Charles Cotton in his addition to Isaac Walton's *The Compleat Angler*, three centuries ago.

During the time of the salmon fly, I have caught trout so gorged that the flies were literally hanging out of their mouths. The term "salmon fly" is applied to the large 2-inch stonefly that appears on Eastern Oregon streams during the spring salmon runs.

The stonefly nymph lives among the rocks and boulders in relatively fast water. It may be a vegetarian or a carnivore. The carnivorous species feed with great gusto on the nymphs of the mayfly and on larvae of caddis flies and midges.

Stonefly nymphs look like mayfly nymphs. Mayfly nymph feet have a single claw, while stoneflies have a pair of them. Virtually all mayfly nymphs have gills extending out from the sides of their abdomens, while those of the stonefly extend from the thorax. The life span under water ranges from one to three years. Stoneflies do not undergo a pupal stage, as do the caddis. Neither do they molt after arriving at wing stage. The change from nymph to winged, apart from acquiring wings, is slight. The mature nymph crawls up a rock, stick, etc., sheds its nymphal skin, and emerges as an adult fly. The stonefly nymph, like the caddis, emerges primarily at night. Its life span is about the same as that of the caddis. They mate on the limbs of trees, on other objects, or on the ground. The female most often deposits eggs while flying. These eggs may be deposited as a single egg-mass or released in small groups; they sink rapidly to the bottom.

Other Aquatic Insects

The Dobson fly and its nymph, the hellgramite, are both attractive food to trout. The nymph is located in the same region as the stonefly. It is never found in great numbers in the West, consequently, is not a major source of food.

The dragonfly and its nymphs find their way occasionally into a trout stomach but are of little importance.

Midges, Blackflies and Punkies (Aquatic Diptera)

Diptera, or true flies, are both aquatic and non-aquatic. The non-aquatic are frequently blown into the water and taken by trout. The mosquito, although aquatic, has its life cycle in stagnant pools, tin cans, etc., and is considered by most fishermen to be a terrestrial insect. It is not an important source of food, although there is a famous fly called the mosquito.

The aquatic diptera in the larval stage are the most important source of trout food in most streams and all lakes. The most important source! This statement by fish biologists really astounds me. These flies consist mainly of midges, tiny blackflies, and punkies, or no-see-ems. When one considers that there have been estimated to be one to two hundreds pounds of insect life per acre of fertile trout stream, there must be an amazing number of diptera larvae on the stream bottom. Because of their size, they are not noticed by fishermen as they hatch. Their relative importance varies from stream to stream. In some, midges are most important, while in others, the blackflies or punkies are most significant. There are also some streams in which diptera are not as important as the mayfly, caddis, or stonefly. These streams are usually soft water and low in lime content, hence not very fertile.

English fly-fishermen call the midge hatch "the curse." This tiny fly hatches in veritable swarms. During such a hatch, trout rise all over a pool. The largest rise of feeding fish I have ever seen has been to a midge hatch at dusk. The midges we commonly associate with these swarms are of a type called non-biting midges. The adult is easily recognized because of its tiny size. There is only one pair of wings, the hind pair being reduced to slender, club-shaped balancing organs. The life cycle consists of the usual egg, larva, pupal, and adult stages. Midge larvae are most abundant in the shallow water areas of lakes, ponds, and streams, favored by a heavy growth of aquatic plants. However, in such areas they are preyed upon more heavily by large insects and fish so that more adult midges may actually emerge from the deeper regions. Like mayflies they do not like sand. The bottom dwellers are found on soft, mucky bottoms; the others, where there is much vegetation such as water weeds, cattails, grasses, etc. The life histories may vary considerably; in warm water there may be a number of generations a year, whereas the same species in a cold lake may require a year or more for emergence.

Midges in the adult stage must be a very tasty dish to produce such tremendous rises of trout. Years ago Edward Hewitt wondered why trout fed so voraciously at times on floating insects. Being an excellent organic chemist, he subjected all types of common aquatic insects to chemical analysis. He found them to be an amazing source of high-protein, high-energy food.

Land-Bred, or Terrestrial, Insects

During the warm months of the spring, summer, and fall, land-bred insects become more important floating feed for trout. At grasshopper time walk in the high grass close to the bank of a stream. This old trick will cause them to jump in the water. Then fish that section of the stream with a hopper fly. You have, in a sense, created your own hatch.

Fly-fishermen on the Letort River in Pennsylvania eagerly await the Japanese beetle invasion, so cursed by the farmers. They tie a special fly to imitate this insect. When the beetle is on the water, this is the insect that the trout prefer above all.

There must be something extra tasty about the flying ant. On trout streams west of the Cascades in Oregon some of the best fly-fishing can be had with the imitation in late April and early May. They seem to prefer this fly partially sunk.

One evening in August I found my favorite Washington cutthroat stream covered with brown moths. I had never seen this before, nor have I seen it since. Fortunately, the fish thought my #10 orange caddis was the same as the moth. I enjoyed a remarkable evening's fishing.

Always keep your eyes open for terrestrials. Who knows, you may run into a swarm of locusts, the seventeen-year type or others. When this occurs in our streams, we frequently get tired releasing fish. Terrestrials . . . the fish and I both love them!

I usually open the stomach of the first trout I catch and examine the contents for predominant nymphs or flies. This is best done by the use of the white china cup and a little water. However, don't rely entirely on this method. Many times a trout's stomach will be gorged with a certain nymph but actually he may have decided to change his bill-of-fare and feed on dry flies. If you try to present to him the nymph found in his stomach, he may ignore it completely.

Until recently, preservation of flies in their natural colors for any long period of time was impossible. The colors faded rapidly in the common preserving solutions made of alcohol, formaldehyde, etc. Now, with the advent of new preserving solutions invented by the Armed Forces Institute of Pathology, this is no longer true. Here is their formula:

Sodium Phosphate Monobasic 8.9 gm.

Sodium Phosphate Dibasic 11.3 gm.

Formaldehyde solution (40%) 95 cc.

Distilled water Q.S. add 190 cc.

Divide this solution in half. Mark them solutions 1 and 2. To solution 2, add sodium hydrosulfite to an extent of 0.5%. As soon as a specimen is captured, place it in solution 1. The specimen will lose most of its color. Allow it to remain in solution 1 for three to seven days, then transfer the specimen to solution 2. This is the solution in which the specimen will be kept permanently. Solution 2 restores the natural color to the specimen. The time that the specimen remains in solution 2 varies. Human tissue, for instance, must remain for at least two weeks.

CHAPTER SIX

Flies

MORE HAS BEEN WRITTEN about flies than about any other aspect of fly-fishing. This preoccupation with flies has prevented many from becoming skillful fishermen. Edward Hewitt emphasized that *only a few fly patterns are necessary to catch the majority of feeding trout*. Flies may be roughly divided into wet and dry. These, in turn, may be classified as imitators, impressionists, and attractors.

Imitators are exact reproductions of the actual insect-larvae or minnow. They are usually made of various plastics and solid materials. In the water they only give off two or three primary colors. The consensus is that they are worthless.

Most of the flies anglers use are *impressionists*. They give the fish the impression of the insect. They are created of natural substances, mainly feathers and fur blended together. An impressionist fly gives off many tiny color waves of various shades and intensity. These blend together to give the same final subtle color effect as produced by the natural fly. A fish rising to a natural fly usually does not stop and inspect it; merely has a momentary impression and seizes it.

The relative importance of size, color, and form is debatable. I feel that size is most important, then color, then form.

Attractor flies are tied of natural material and usually do not imitate any known insect. They are a combination of bright colors that attract and even excite fish. The Royal Coachman is the most famous and probably the greatest, especially when there is no insect hatch on the water. The bulk of the flies used for anadromous fish are attractors.

From this point on we will disregard imitators and be concerned only with impressionists and attractors.

Dry flies are fished on top of the water and wet flies beneath. The construction is guided by this. However, a dry fly may be used as a wet fly and vice versa. Fig. 16 depicts most of the varieties of wet and dry fly. A quick appraisal reveals the standard dry fly has upright wings and a round hackle while the standard wet fly has a slanting wing and a flat hackle. Most of these flies are tied primarily to represent impressionistically May and Caddis flies. I use very few standard wet flies. In their place I find most dry flies work as well.

The beginning fly fisherman, when confronted with a catalog from one of the stores that specializes in flies, becomes hopelessly confused. Fig. 16 is an attempt to bring order out of confusion.

Dry Flies

1. *Standard divided-wing dry fly:* See brief description above.
2. *Fan-wing:* A dry fly with large wings; the emphasis is on the wings. This fly, which probably represents a spent spinner, is popular on the East Coast.
3. *Spent-wing:* Represents a spent spinner. The wings are usually tied with hackle tips. The emphasis, again, is on the wings.
4. *Hackle fly:* My favorite; exactly like the standard dry fly

Fig. 16. Flies.

except without wings. Like many other fishermen I do not feel the wings contribute anything but looks to a low- or clear-water dry fly. I especially like these because they are easier to tie.

5. *Variant:* A fly with large hackles, out of proportion to the wing and hook. These flies supposedly represent a high-floating dun.

6. *Spider:* Similar to a *variant*, but without wings. The hackles are even larger in proportion to the hook.

7. *Bivisible:* Invented by the late Edward Hewitt. Good for both high- and low-water conditions; floats well in rough water; bivisible because the white front hackle makes it visible to the fisherman as well as to the fish. The hackle extends the entire length of the hook; this is referred to as Palmer-tied. Many claim that the brown and gray bivisible in various sizes is the only fly necessary to catch trout on a dry fly. This fly works equally well as a wet fly.

8. *Bucktail:* With wings made of bucktail, these represent large caddis and stoneflies. When these flies are on the water they work well in high- or low-water conditions. This is a dual-purpose fly. When fished wet as a streamer fly, it represents minnows as well as caddis and stoneflies. The illustration is tied with dry fly fishing in mind.

9. *Divided hair-wing or Wulff type fly:* My favorite high- or rough-water dry fly. The bucktail or hair-wing gives this fly excellent floating characteristics. Fished wet and pulled against the current, the wings pulsate, giving an enticing action. This type is primarily for dry fly fishing.

10. *Tied-down-bucktail:* Popularly referred to as a tied-down caddis, for some reason this variety is at times more effective than a regular bucktail. When fished wet, it looks like a caddis nymph.

11. *Woolly worm:* A Palmer-tied fly on a long shank hook, tied to represent a caterpillar. Fished wet, I suspect it also represents a stonefly nymph. Popular in Colorado and Montana streams; also works well on the West Coast.

12. *Parachute fly:* See Fig. 17. The variety I prefer was perfected by Lloyd Byerly of Portland, Oregon, who has invented

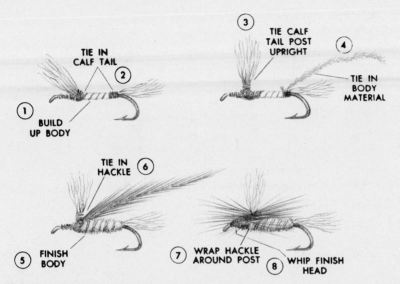

Fig. 17. Buszek's Parachute (by Byerly).

a simple method of tying this excellent floater. Lloyd feels that trout heavily fished over become accustomed to the standard dry fly, and so a different-appearing fly will entice them when standards will not. All standard patterns may be tied as parachute flies. The post in the center is usually tied with white calf tail, which enhances visibility. Wet, this fly looks like a nymph. Parachute flies are excellent in both high and low water. I use this fly for about 60 percent of my dry fly fishing.

Wet Flies

1. *Standard wet fly:* See previous description on page 00.
2. *Hackle fly:* This is similar to the hackle fly shown under dry flies, except that in this case the hackles are frequently tied with soft hen hackles instead of gamecock hackles. Hackles usually slant backwards. You will frequently hear the term nymph fly used. These are finely tied hackle flies and were popularized in this country by James Leisenring.

3. *Nymphs:* This variety comes the closest to being an accurate imitation. The blending of natural materials in its construction prevents it from being classified as a true imitator. There is a controversy among experts in this field as to which represents the natural nymph the best, the nymph fly or the nymph.

4. *Streamer:* Similar to the classic wet fly, but with longer wings. Represents minnows, young trout, and salmon. Many are tied as attractor flies. Wings may be tied with feathers, bucktail, or maribou.

5. *Divided-wing bucktail:* Popular on the Rogue River for summer steelhead, this fly is usually tied without hackles. The wing slants back more than the Wulff-type dry fly. They are usually tied as attractor flies.

6. *Classic English salmon fly (heavy-water variety):* These are complex-tied flies for Atlantic salmon. When tied in proper patterns, they work equally well for steelhead.

7. *Classic English salmon fly (low-water variety):* Similar to the classic English heavy-water variety, except it is lightly tied.

Fly Selection

Selection of patterns should be guided by the locality one desires to fish. A good native fly fisherman or local fly shop can be of inestimable help in fly selection. A cardinal point to remember is that *a few patterns of various sizes are preferable to a great many patterns all of the same size.*

It is possible to have a selection of flies that will catch the majority of feeding trout throughout the entire United States. In selecting this list I have kept in mind high- and low-water conditions or, expressed in another manner, rough and clear water. Remember, heavily tied flies are used for heavy water, lightly tied flies are used for clear water. Any of the flies described under the column as clear-water flies may be tied with hair wings and heavy hackle to become heavy water flies.

DRY FLIES (CLEAR WATER)

*Quill-Gordon—18, 14, 10; smoky gray
*Adams—18, 14, 10; gray-brown
*Light Cahill—18, 14, 10; light, yellow-brown
March Brown—14, 10; brown
*Red Upright—14, 19; red-brown
Olive Dun—14, 10; olive
Black Gnat—14, 10; black
*Brown Spider—12

The three patterns selected in size 18—Quill Gordon, Adams, and Light Cahill—should be tied as hackle flies without wings. These represent midges in this size. The flies marked with an asterisk (*) are in my opinion the most essential patterns for dry-fly fishing. If limited to one size, choose #14.

DRY FLIES (HEAVY WATER)

*Bucktail Royal Coachman—12; red and white
*Irresistible—12; gray-brown
*Muddler Minnow—10; brown
Gray Wulff—12; gray
White Wulff—12; white

NYMPHS AND NYMPH FLIES

*Gray Nymph—10, 14; gray
*Ed Burke—12, 14; black
*Birdstone Salmon fly nymph—8; brown with orange overtones
*Atherton Medium—12, 14; gray brown
*Olive Mayfly nymph—12, 14; olive

STREAMER FLIES

*Bucktail Royal Coachman—10, 8
*Mickey Finn—10, 8; orange and red
*Gray Ghost—10, 8; gray
Black-nosed Dace—10, 8
Rainbow—10, 8

If limited to one size, choose #10.

CHOOSING THE PROPER FLY

The choice of the proper dry fly is quite simple. Select the fly from your box that comes closest to the size, color, and shape that appears (or should appear) on the water.

Wet fly fishing is more demanding in its fly requirements. A knowledge of local stream entomology is a tremendous help. A few minutes spent kicking rocks will help you decide on the proper nymph or wet fly.

Streamer fly fishing will always be a trial-and-error technique, especially with the attractor streamers that make up 80 percent of all streamer fishing. Local lore is of paramount importance. The Royal Coachman seems to work everywhere.

Leader Selection

The size of the fly you select and the condition of the water determine the size of your leader. Much has been written about leader color. I have never noted any difference between natural monofilament or gut and the stained variety, as far as the number of fish caught is concerned. The big factor is the size of gut.

Fine, long leaders for clear, low water and small flies; coarser leaders and larger flies for rough and colored water.

The shortest leaders I ever use are nine feet and the longest about twelve feet. Some nymph fishermen use leaders as long as twenty feet. In dry and wet fly fishing the commonest size is a 4X—nine-foot leader for size 14 and 12 flies; 5X for size 16 and midges; 2X for size 8 and 6 wet flies.

Flies have become more and more expensive in the past few years as inflation takes its toll. The only way to beat the cost of flies is to learn to tie your own. I have seldom met a skillful fly-fisherman who at some time did not tie his own flies. I take a fly-tying kit with me on extended fishing trips, especially in new country. Being able to tie the right fly has many times meant the difference between the proper fly and fish, and no fish.

Many years ago, I was privileged to spend some time with

the late Edward Hewitt, inventor of the bivisible fly and author of numerous books on fly-fishing for trout and salmon. Mr. Hewitt, who was in his eighties at the time, showed me some flies he had tied. They were just as sloppy as mine and made me feel better. The beauty and neatness of a fly is not the important factor. Many fly-tiers tie bushy flies that are beautiful to look at but will not catch fish as well as a sloppy but sparsely tied one. Most people tie too much wing and hackle on their flies.

Flies are fascinating and fun to experiment with, but they are third in importance to reading water and proper fly presentation. In your fishing career, if you will emphasize these two factors, you will catch many more fish than the man who emphasizes flies and fly patterns.

CHAPTER SEVEN

Wading

IT HAS BEEN SAID that 10 percent of the fishermen catch 90 percent of the fish. It is true that 90 percent of the fishermen wade when they should not. There seems to be an irresistible urge for the novice to get into the water, a situation somewhat analogous to the small boy and the mud puddle. There are three basic reasons for wading:

1. To present the fly properly. As an example, overhanging tree limbs prevent a roll or side cast from the shore to a likely area.

2. The stream is too wide, and wading is the only way the fisherman can reach a likely spot. In many instances, however, a fisherman mistakenly wades through good fishing water to cast to an obvious spot. Obvious fishing spots can be seen and fished by everyone, hence usually contain few fish. The out-of-the-way pockets and riffles are especially productive; these account for the expert's success.

3. The fisherman's presence may be too obvious when he stands on the bank. An example of this is Silver Creek in Idaho.

When certain conditions prevail, this river is winding, slow-moving, full of moss or water plants. The water level is practically even with the soft, spongy bank. Any step can be felt by a trout for a great distance. In this situation the fisherman is also silhouetted against the sky. By wading close to the bank he is much less visible. Depending on the speed of the current, walking upstream sends vibrations only a few feet upstream. I have hooked fish as close as 6 feet from me and have had them rise to a natural fly at my elbow. If you must wade, do it slowly, quietly, and carefully. I have put more fish down by wading carelessly than I have ever caught.

Every fisherman should perform this experiment at least once. Go at least 100 to 200 feet below a wading fisherman. Put your head under water and listen. The racket is astounding! Downstream wading must be done in a slow, pause-and-wait fashion.

The footwork used in wading is similar to that used in boxing. The angler goes forward or retreats with one foot always advanced. Standing with both feet close together while wading is an invitation to a swim.

Wading staffs are a nuisance, but in very fast water they can mean the difference between a wet and dry angler. A long, light aluminum ski pole with the basket removed makes a dandy wading staff. A short rope should link the handle and the fisherman's belt to allow the staff to hang free when fishing. I personally find a new wooden pole every time I need one and discard it when I have finished using it. On the average big stream, one seldom uses the staff more than two or three times in a day's fishing.

Any fisherman who wades in water above his thighs and does not wear some form of life preserver is a damn fool. I too had to learn this the hard way. There are several fishing vests on the market today that incorporate a rubber bladder, which can be inflated by a CO_2 cartridge. Keep about a quart of air in the bladder. You know then that it does not leak and the amount of air contributes some buoyancy until you can pull the lanyard that releases the CO_2.

If you fish long enough, you are bound to slip and be forced to swim. Don't panic! Keep your feet down and tread water. Go with the current. Bounce your feet on the bottom, if possible, and at the same time angle in toward shore. Usually it is impossible to swim back to the spot from which you started. A great deal of strength is wasted trying to do so. If you are caught in a large rapid with numerous boulders, assume a sitting position and put your feet in front of you to act as a bumper. The Navy teaches their frogmen to come through a rocky surf in this manner.

There has been a great deal of nonsense written about waders and hipboots pulling the fisherman down. Archimedes' principle disproves this. Personally, I wear a belt around my waders. In case of a fall it helps to keep the water out and it prevents the trapping of air. Much has been said pro and con the possibility of waders trapping air and turning the luckless fisherman over to float downstream head down. It can happen! It happened to me! I was standing too close to a ledge, and both feet suddenly went out from under me. As I went over backward, my waders trapped air, and I floated downstream upside-down. I panicked but finally managed to right myself in about four feet of water. My partner, Bronc Choate, nearly fell in laughing.

Choice of wading equipment is a problem. Most use hipboots with attached rubber feet . . . preferably with felt soles. Pieces of carpet glued on with Pliobond (Goodyear) do as well.

Waist-high waders present a real problem. Stocking-foot waders with separate wading shoes are lighter, slightly easier to walk in, dry out faster, and are more expensive. Once you own them they are hard to get rid of. First, the waders wear out and you still have good shoes. Then you purchase a new pair of waders and then the shoes wear out . . . this goes on endlessly!

I prefer rubberboot-foot waders. They are easier to take on and off, and are warmer and cheaper. During the course of the day's fishing, I like to stop and rest and remove my waders. I personally can walk in them as well as the stockingfoot waders with wading shoes.

Again, I repeat . . . DON'T wade without a life preserver! If you are unfortunate enough to get into trouble without a preserver, don't panic. Waders will not pull you under. Go with the current and all will be well. I know! I have done it both ways more than once.

COMMON ERRORS IN FLY FISHING

1. Slurping the fly from the water because of dissatisfaction with a cast.
2. More than three false casts.
3. Over-wading.
4. Too-bushy flies.

PART II

Stream Tactics

CHAPTER EIGHT

First Trip

T HE PART OF THIS book that deals with fundamentals is finished. It is now a good time to take several trips together to demonstrate practical stream tactics, in various seasons, to fish for rainbow and brown trout.

It is a lovely sunny June day. There was a heavy rain about one week ago and the stream is at its ideal, midseason water level; not high and not low.

We arrive at the oval pool (Plate 2, Fig. 18), at 8:00 A.M. With the exception of very hot weather late in the season, I have seldom had good fishing much before 8:00 A.M. Mr. Biddle even claimed that he caught more fish around noon than at any other time.

A few blue duns can be seen rising from the water. Let's rig up! We will both fish dry flies with floating lines, and 9-foot 4X leaders. I will use a #14 Blue Upright and you a #14 Quill Gordon. They both represent essentially the same fly.

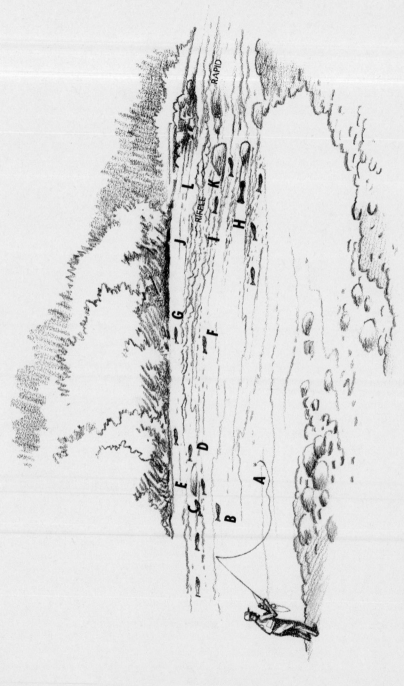

Fig. 18. Oval pool.

Plate 2.

This pool is about 100 feet long and about 50 feet wide; a small pool. Although it is an oval pool, there is no slack water in the mid-portion as there is in most oval pools. You know, oval pools occur primarily in small streams; pools in large streams usually have a curve in them.

We will start fishing at the tail of this pool and work upstream. Our first location will be on the left side. Note that the water is flowing from right to left. Put your first cast at about point A.

The fly came down beautifully. Now bring in line as it drifts toward you. There is too much slack in your line. That's better . . . you have just the right amount of slack now. Bring it in slowly, roll-cast it off the water, and cast it to point B. Still no rise? Your next cast should place the fly just behind that rock at point C.

You broke the fly off in the fish's mouth! There was too much arm in your strike! When you have a short line without much slack, just use your wrist; use your arm and your wrist when you have a lot of slack line. Tie on another Quill Gordon; now cast to point D just ahead of that rock. You hooked one! It's a beauty—it must be 16 inches long! Reel in the slack in your hand and get the fish on your reel. Now he's going to jump! Lower the tip a bit and give him some slack. He's still on but he's getting tired; see him turn on his side? Be sure to net him head-first, otherwise he might swim out of the net. Good catch!

Next, cast to point E on the other side of the rock. You missed that rise! You struck too late because you did not use enough arm when you struck against all that slack line. Now try a cast to the edge of the bushes.

I'll let you decide where to make your next cast. To point I? Wrong! If you do that, you will have to cast over all that good water at points F and G, which will put any fish down. Try F and G first, and then I.

I'm going to leave you now and explore a little bit. I'll be back in a few minutes. Be sure to fish H, J, K, and L in that order.

As we fished in the preceding paragraphs we utilized the

quartering upstream presentation of Chapter 3, the *commonest method of fishing the dry fly.*

You are now standing on the second fishing spot, as indicated in Fig. 18. Notice that it has not been necessary to wade to present your fly properly. Last week I found one poor fellow standing in the middle of this pool at point F, casting to the opposite shore. He did not realize that he was standing right in some of the best water. I have seen this happen time after time.

We are going to change our tactics. Put your fly in your mouth and moisten it. I know it is a dry fly, but we are going to fish it as a wet one. First, cast directly below to point H. Sink the fly by pulling it under and then bring it back slowly with little twitches of the rod tip in order to give the fly a swimming motion. Now, cast to K and repeat the procedure. You are fishing the most productive water, namely, where the fast and slow water meet. Cast your fly in progressive stages to I and G. Each time, your fly will swing around into the smooth water area on your side. When it finishes its swing, allow the fly to pause for at least thirty seconds or a minute. Then strip off a few feet of line and let the fly drift back a foot or two, then bring it in with little twitches.

The above is the quartering down and across stream presentation in Chapter 3, page 30, the commonest method of fishing the wet fly.

When you started fishing this pool with a curved upstream cast, you could have allowed the fly to swing around on each cast until it was quartering downstream. Then, giving an extra hard jerk, you could sink the fly and fish it as a wet fly. *This is the wet-dry method with a combination of the curved upstream and the quartering downstream presentation.*

In a short pool like this it is possible to fish the entire pool, using a long line, with a downstream wet-dry method from position 2, and never use the upstream technique. Cast first to the nearest water, where the fast and slow water meet, as shown in points H and F, then cast to the farthest waters. Don't make the common mistake of overfishing the water.

If you are fishing the dry fly in the wet fashion and you see a trout rise to a natural fly, bring your fly in, blot it with a dry handkerchief, then re-apply mucilin. *Voila!* You are again ready to cast a dry fly.

Having decimated this pool of its fish population, let us now proceed to the curved pool.

Curved Pool and Deflector

The section of river depicted in Plate 3, Fig. 19, reveals two basic pools. We are looking upstream; the water is flowing toward us. The pool at our feet, produced by two sunken logs extending diagonally out into the current, is a beautiful example of a pool formed by a deflector. The pool above this, where the big log has fallen into the water, is a good example of a large, curved pool.

We will fish the deflector pool first. Here is a situation we must wade to fish properly. We will walk directly out about 6 feet from where the picture was taken, just far enough to clear the brush with our back-cast. The water here is just below our knees.

Start casting at A, then cast to B near the end of the log, next to C, and then in the sequence as indicated by the letters to cover the entire water. Don't forget to bring in the slack as your fly drifts back to you.

A large trout just rose to your fly and turned back before taking it. Why? You have the correct pattern, but it is too large. Change from a #12 Blue Upright to a #14 and try again. You've hooked a beauty! He is tired now and on his side; bring him gently up to you. Reach down with your cupped hand and lift up under his belly. Now there is no net and line to untangle. Just take the hook out and gently return him. Once you have a firm grasp on a trout's belly, he usually stops struggling. Most of the truly skillful trout fishermen I have known never bother with a net. When they land a fish, they either catch it in their hands or, if it's too large, beach it.

Let's climb back on the bank and go up to the curved pool. You will see pools ike this many times. It is big, and we can waste a lot of time fishing non-productive water. Above the deflector logs is a long rapids. It looks fishable in the picture, but the water is really too fast and too shallow. There is not enough protection for either rainbow or brown trout. Just above this is the region of the break, where in the evening you will occasionally find native trout. It is also a location in which sea-run fish—such as salmon, steelhead, and cut-throat trout—like to lie. If proper gravel is present, it is the commonest spawning area.

We could now go up the left side of the pool, fishing primarily between the fast and smooth water. This is the most obvious tactic, however, and exactly the same situation we encountered in the last pool. Consequently, we are going to find two stout poles and wade across to the other side. We will start just in front of us and go directly across. Check your life vest and let's go!

From the break on up, the water to the right is about 8 feet deep. We are not going to find a location for trout until we reach a small pocket of reverse current or back-eddy water (point H). This is a spot often neglected by the average fisherman. Here are big fish. The water is still deep, but there is a natural collecting place for food. How are we going to approach this? The bank is steep. We will walk to fishing point 2 located 6 feet downstream from the back-eddy. Another location is fishing point 3 on top of the bank. We could use point 3 if the bank is too steep to stand on, but this is the least preferable location. First, there is the difficulty of presenting the fly; second is the possibility of the trout seeing us silhouetted against the sky.

You see those tiny flies starting to appear on the water? We are about to experience a midge hatch. It is about the right time of the evening for one to appear. We'll either have tremendous fishing or be completely frustrated. The English call such a hatch "the curse." The size and color of your flies are of paramount importance in fishing a midge hatch. A #20 hook

Fig. 19. Curve and deflector pool.

Plate 3.

will do for the size. We will ascertain the color by dipping a
few midges from the water. They are a dark gray-blue. Unless
one can reasonably match the color as well as the size of the
insects, few fish will be hooked. We must now change our
leader. We can do two things—put on 9-foot 5X leader or tie a
5X tippet to our present 4X leader, by adding about 12 inches
of 5X nylon with a blood knot to the end of the leader. This
makes a 10-foot leader that will fish better than a 9-foot 5X
leader. Be sure and stretch it well, so that it will lie straight
on the water.

Make your first cast upstream to the edge of the eddy. Now
the midges are really swarming, and our back-eddy pocket is
boiling with big fish. You have had five good strikes and no
hooked fish; that's par for the course. If you can land one or
two big fish in an hour's fishing, you're doing well. You must
admit that at least there is plenty of action.

Well, we have fished for about an hour and have three fish
between us. It's beginning to get dark and the midges have
departed as rapidly as they appeared. It is time to return to
camp.

*The fly presentation used in fishing the back-eddy from posi-
tion 2 is the directly upstream cast (Chapter 3, page 30).*

CHAPTER NINE

Opening Day

CUT-BANK POOLS

T HE NEXT TRIP will be on the opening day of the season. We are going to fish the cut-bank pool illustrated in Plate 4, Fig. 20. Deforestation has made this river one of great fluctuations. Sometimes it floods to such an extent that most of the native browns and rainbows are destroyed along with their spawning beds. Consequently, it is heavily stocked with hatchery inno-cents. The river today is moderately high, relatively clear, and very cold. The water temperature is in the region of 46 to 48 degrees. I have been warned that there have been no hatches for the past week. Two weeks ago, during a warm spell, a few Quill Gordons were seen, but since then there have been prac-tically no flies. This will be a wet fly situation. I am going to use my version of a Bumble Puppy . . . a streamer originally tied by Theodore Gordon to represent a minnow. I would suggest you use my all-time favorite, a #10 Bucktail Royal Coachman. We will use our sinking lines and fish this pool in the classic wet fly method, using the quartering downstream cast.

Fig. 20. Cutbank pool.

Plate 4.

The pool is about 5 feet deep over by the cut-bank and along most of its length. There is a strong, relatively slow current. Because of the cold weather, the fish are apt to be against the cut-bank, deep down, in the middle portions of the pool. The bank slopes gradually to the river, with plenty of room for our back-casts.

We will start fishing at a point upstream, outside the picture, standing at least 10 feet from the water's edge. Cast your fly to A, B, and C in that order, then walk gingerly to fishing location 2.

Now wait a minute before you start casting to D, E, F, and G. Up until this point you have presented your fly only at the middle layer of the stream. These fish are probably resting on the bottom. You have used a quartering downstream cast and allowed your fly to sweep around to a position below you. Now cast upstream to A, B, and C with a curved upstream cast. This will allow your fly to sink to a deeper level. When the line is parallel to you, strip off several feet. This will slow your fly down and allow it to sink deeper. When the line has reached a 45 degree angle below you, strip off several more feet; your cast will be extended and your fly will slow down again to remain deep for a bit longer. Do not strip off line too fast, because you should fish with a tight line during the downstream phase. When fishing a wet fly, try to fish all the layers of the water.

I have a suggestion. You fished your fly with no action. At times, trout want a wet fly without any action; at other times, they want action. Most wet-fly fishermen fish their flies without action until they reach an angle of 60 degrees below them, at which point they start to pump or twitch their flies. Sometimes it is a good idea to pump the fly from the very beginning of the cast, varying the pumping action from small twitches to large jerks.

We have combined the curved upstream and the quartering downstream casts. This can also be used with the dry fly.

Now it's my turn. The sun has come out and warmed up the water; if we were to take the surface temperature I think it would be around 50 degrees. A few Quill Gordons are hatching.

I am going to show you an unorthodox method of fishing a dry fly. Each year I fish this method more and more. I am going to use my sinking line and fish a dry fly. I will prepare my Quill Gordon with mucilin. The cast will be as usual for dry-fly fishing, with an upstream curved line and no drag. Watch carefully! The fly will float naturally until it reaches a point about 45 degrees below me. By this time the middle portion of the sinking line will be down about 2 or 3 feet, depending on the length of the cast. Drag has now developed; I will pull the fly under and, from this point on, fish a sunk wet fly in the middle layer of the water.

At one time I was foolish enough to think that this was a private discovery of my own. However, Sid Gordon writes of it in his book, *How to Fish from Top to Bottom*, as does Lee Wulff in his book, *Atlantic Salmon*. It also works well with fly fishing in trout lakes.

Again, we have combined the curved upstream and quartering downstream casts.

It is your turn to try another unorthodox method. Change your line to a floating variety. Tie a dropper roughly 4 inches in length about 4 feet from the tip of the leader (see Fig. 8, page 31). Tie a wet fly or a streamer to the tip of the leader. Tie a dry fly on the dropper. Moisten the wet fly at the tip of the leader with saliva, glycerin, soap, or some other wetting agent. Use mucilin on the dry fly attached to the dropper. Fish this rig exactly as you would a dry fly. The tip fly should be 2 to 3 inches under the water and the dropper fly will ride as a conventional fly. This method is especially effective when nymphs are rising to the surface. I have had equally good results using a large streamer as the tip fly. Many times I have caught doubles, using this arrangement.

I'll sit on the bank and watch you.

You fished that well. There is, however, one technique you could have added. You initially used the curved upstream cast, allowed both flies to drift past you until they started to drag, then pulled them both under and fished them back as conventional wet flies. I find no fault with this technique. There are times, though, when you will want to use it with a nymph or a dry fly in place of the streamer at the end of the leader. In this situation you might extend the natural drift downstream as far as you can. When your flies start to drag, instead of pulling them under and fishing them as wet flies, put a small mend in your line to continue the natural drift. The downstream belly that formed in your line caused the drag. By mending it you produce an upstream belly. You may have to mend your line two or three times in the course of one drift.

We Americans do not use the line mend often enough. English fishermen are masters of it. It is essential for any technique that requires naturally drifting flies, either on top of or beneath the water. However, one word of caution: I have seen fishermen so entranced with line mending that they did it unnecessarily and too frequently, thereby putting fish down with the disturbance of their line.

Before we separate and move on to other pools I want to review what we have done in this pool. First, you fished, quartering down and across with a sinking line; then you used a curved upstream cast and free drift to sink your line down well; when the fly was opposite you, you stripped the line slowly from your reel and again when it was 45 degrees below you. During this time, you maintained a relatively tight line so that you could feel a fish strike.

Then I used the same technique with a dry fly and a sinking line. The first half of the cast I fished as a conventional curved upstream cast with free-floating dry fly. Then, when the fly began to drag, I pulled it under and fished it as a quartering downstream sunken fly, with a tight line.

Finally, you changed to a floating line. We discussed mending the line, using a floating line, and fishing a fly with a natural drift throughout. These are the variations of combined upstream and quartering downstream casts. These variations make up a tremendous part of the essence of fly fishing.

Let us walk downstream to the next pool.

SHALLOW RIFFLE

We have now reached a large, relatively fast, shallow riffle located between two pools. We are looking upstream at the head of this riffle, illustrated in Plate 5, Fig. 21. The water averages 3 to 4 feet in depth. There are medium-sized, well-covered rocks scattered throughout the water. Below us the

Fig. 21. Shallow riffle.

Plate 5.

riffle is too fast to contain many fish, so we will not spend any time fishing it. For 50 feet in front of us there is slow-moving water, then it blends with the fast water. Again, there is a definite visible junction between the two currents.

Early in the season brown and rainbow trout will inhabit a shallow riffle on sunny days because of the combination of the food and the water. The sun's rays going through the shallow water produce a warming effect much sooner than is felt in deeper water. The rocky bottom is a favorite habitat for the nymphs of the mayfly and stonefly all during the season. A hatch will develop here long before it starts in other parts of the stream.

The floating line you are fishing with is especially suitable for this stretch. Change the front fly to a Gray Nymph; the dropper fly remains dry. Fish the dry fly and the nymph in the usual dry-fly manner. Use an upstream curved cast. I will sit on the bank while you fish. The area between A and B, where the fast and slow currents join, is a very productive region, as usual. The fish will be scattered throughout, so be sure to fish well into the riffle (C, D, and E).

You have been fishing fifteen minutes and I have counted five rises to your front nymph. Trout will usually not hook themselves on a naturally floating nymph. You must strike quickly when a trout rises to your sunken nymph, in exactly the same manner as with a dry fly. Nymph fishing is underwater dry-fly fishing. Usually you have to see the fish rise in order to hook him. This is a fact glossed over by most writers who describe nymph fishing. There is another method, using a weighted nymph deep, which we will discuss later.

Clean your fish as you catch them so that you will not have the problem of spoiled fish at the day's end. While you are cleaning that last fish, I will tell you a few more facts about shallow riffles.

Mid-day, late in the season, with temperatures at hot summer levels, trout will not be found in shallow riffles. They become wary and do not like the exposed position; also, the water temperature has become too high for their liking. Then

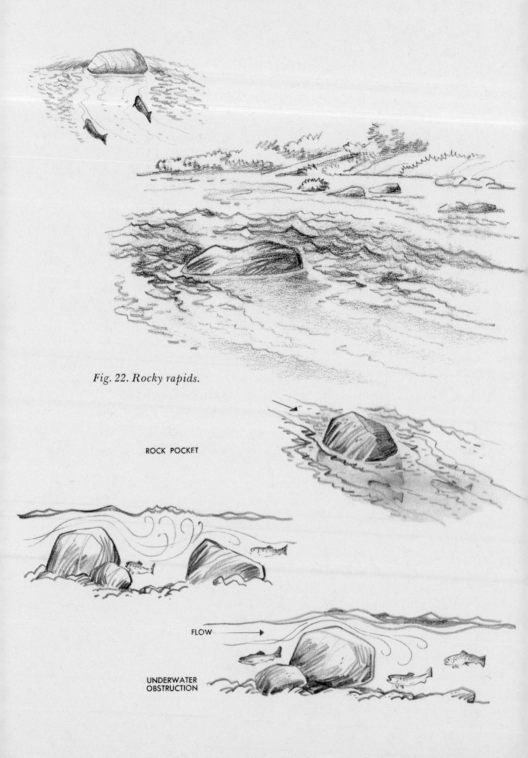

Fig. 22. Rocky rapids.

ROCK POCKET

FLOW

UNDERWATER
OBSTRUCTION

Plate 6.

Plate 7.

they occupy shallow riffles at dusk, where it is more difficult to see them and the water is cooler.

ROCKY RAPIDS

Slow down! You are about to pass up some of the best water on the stream! Yes, the fast rapids (depicted in Plates 6 and 7, Fig. 22) have big fish in them. Most fishermen pass up these rapids as too fast to hold trout. The secret lies in those big rocks jutting up. Trout lie directly behind these rocks and in the slick extending 6 to 10 feet downstream. At times they also lie in the cushion of slow water directly in front of the rocks. If the water is not too fast, they will even lie at the sides. The water here is 3 to 4 feet deep. Check your life preserver. The river can knock you off your feet and you might end up in the suck-holes and whirlpools in the treacherous deep pool below.

The first rock you are going to fish is seen in Plate 6. Use your conventional dry-fly outfit, floating line, 9-foot 2X or 3X leader. A heavier leader is necessary here because the fish usually swim out in the fast current, and a light leader will break. Furthermore, the water is turbulent, and the heavier leader will not show as much as it would in slow water. Tie on a #10 Irresistible. This is one of my favorite heavy-water flies. It has a clipped hair body and hair wings, the same coloration as the Adams fly. It is tied so heavily that it looks like a bass bug and can be used for that purpose.

Wade out 20 feet directly below the rock. Cast into the tail end of the slick and then gradually extend your cast until your fly lands against the rock, then cast your fly close to each side of the rock.

It is easy to lose big trout in this water; therefore you must let the fish run even if it goes down into the next pool. That's why you have a hundred yards of 10-pound monofilament back-ing on your reel. You must play these big fish from the reel exactly as you would a steelhead or a salmon. More big fish are lost on the initial run than at any other time. Usually, on reaching that big pool below, they will make a jump. When they do, lower the tip of your rod. This will help to prevent the hook from being torn out of the fish's mouth.

Next, wade to a point just opposite the rock, about 30 feet out. Tie on a weighted mayfly nymph and cast it directly behind the rock. Allow it to drift directly through the swift water without drag.

No luck? Now wade slowly and carefully to a point directly above the rock. Rest that water for at least ten minutes. Now tie on a #10 Bucktail Stonefly. First, fish it as a downstream dry fly along both sides of the rock, and then into the slick. When you bring it back, try to ease it on top of the water and pull it through the slick with little twitches. At times this will drive trout crazy; at other times it will put them down. A bouncing spider fly is particularly deadly with this technique. Both techniques work well at times. The spider fly will work better in clear, calm water.

Still no luck? Put a split shot at the head of your fly. Remember, there is not much difference in appearance between a stonefly nymph and a stonefly. Sunken, it looks like the nymph, especially in fast water. Now, fish it through the slick as you would a streamer.

A weighted fly is a lethal weapon; when you fish a weighted fly, wear a hat and a pair of Polaroid glasses. Had Ambassador Lewis Douglas worn a pair, while fishing on a Scottish salmon river, he probably would not have lost an eye when it was struck by a weighted fly.

ROCKY REACH

Upstream from here is a beautiful rocky reach (Plate 8, Fig. 23). What is a rocky reach? The word "reach" is an English term loosely applied to a fishable stretch of water lying between two well-defined pools. The water may be fast, slow, full of rocks, etc. It conjures up the picture of an English gentleman, complete with tweed knickers and cap, fishing Lord Havershaw's Reach on the River Spa with his gilly waiting patiently just behind him. I have always wanted a gilly but I don't know

Fig. 23. Rocky reach.

Plate 8.

what I'd do with him . . . have him carry the beer? Or make excuses for my fishing?

This stretch could best be defined as a shallow, rocky reach. On a bright day such as this, the fish often lie in the shadows of the rocks, close in at their sides. The water is relatively slow and clear. I would suggest that you use a long line (a minimum of 30 feet; 50 feet is better) and a light 5X leader. Remember, the longer the line that you can use practically, the more chance you have of catching big, wary fish. Err on the side of too long a cast. If you can see a fish, he usually can see you!

Fish this in exactly the same manner that you did the Rocky Rapids . . . except for a long line.

CHAPTER TEN

Some Things Easily Missed

HIDDEN POOL (PRACTICAL NYMPH FISHING)

THE NEXT SECTION of the stream we shall fish consists of a pool that can be easily missed unless the fisherman is alert to its possibilities. Above and below this pool are two large, typical, deep curved pools. Both are obvious and are fished very heavily. Between these two pools is a straight stretch of shallow, fast rapids averaging 1 to 2 feet in depth and about 80 feet in width. As we walk down this stretch and reach a point about midway between the two large pools, we will notice an area where the water becomes darker in appearance and the rate of flow slightly slower (Plate 9). A careful scrutiny reveals a shallow pool, about 75 feet long. From the spot on which we are standing the bottom slopes downward until it reaches a maximum depth of about 5 feet approximately 2 feet from the opposite shore. The bank on the opposite shore is very

Plate 9.

steep but is not undercut. To fish this stretch from the other shore is difficult, almost impossible. It is not practical to wade upstream. To stand on the bank and cast any distance upstream is out of the question because of the shrubbery on the edge of the bank. Floating a long line downstream with many 'S' curves is possible but very difficult. Most of the trout in this stream will know you are there by the vibration you set up as you attempt to fish downstream. The most deadly manner in which to fish this area is from the side we are standing on.

About 10 feet behind us are pine trees so we must wade out about 20 feet to have enough room for a back-cast. It is true that a good roll-caster might stand on the edge of the bank and cast across, but in this situation the longer the line, the quicker it will develop drag. I want you to fish this first with a dry fly. Start fishing and gradually work your fly across to the opposite bank; then move upstream and repeat.

No fish! And no evident fly hatch. We are going to have to change our tactics. Before we do this, however, I want to re-emphasize what a deadly technique is fishing from one bank to the other. This is what makes boat fishing so effective. The ability to float slowly downstream and cast to either shore will often produce fish when bank fishermen have nothing for their pains but empty creels.

Our present situation requires a deeply sunk nymph. Come sit on the bank with me and we will discuss nymph and nymph fly fishing. All the techniques we have discussed in this book on fly presentation apply to nymph fishing. You can even grease one of these flies and fish it as a dry fly. Don't forget that a mayfly nymph floats on the surface while the dun is breaking out of its shell.

Most nymph flies and nymphs are tied on heavy hooks. These are nothing but standard hooks made of thicker wire. They will sink somewhat faster than conventional hooks. Commonly, the nymph is fished under water, without drag, in exactly the same manner as the dry fly. It should be fished in varying water depths. The true nymph experts fish with a 9- or 12-foot sinking leader and a floating line.

There is one major problem in nymph fishing—getting the nymph down! This form of fishing is most effective on slow-moving brown trout streams. I am convinced that the brown trout is a better taker of nymphs than his cousin the rainbow. Many Eastern brown trout experts, fishing in private club waters, will locate a large brown trout in such water and then, after much thought, organize a deliberate campaign, stalking the fish and catching him with a nymph.

Enough talk! This is a rainbow stream. The current in the hidden pool is not too swift to fish a nymph in the conventional manner. You sit on the bank as I demonstrate.

I will wade out as you did before. I have cast quartering upstream. The nymph-and-leader is now sinking. I judge that it is about 3 feet underwater. Now it is opposite me and I will gradually lift it out of the water. Wham! I have hooked one—old Leisenring's technique worked. The fish was a beauty but he is off now. He certainly stirred up this pool. I will sit down and rest it for a spell.

The lift I used was originated by the late Jim Leisenring, who perfected nymph flies. At any time in the drift of the nymph one simply raises the fly rod upward; this makes the nymph rise deliberately to the surface. This maneuver imitates natural nymphs rising to the surface to hatch. It is very difficult to perform this maneuver in fast water.

How do you get a nymph down in fast water? Use a nymph tied with a lead wire body. They are miserable things to cast and lose their lifelike qualities when floating in the water.

The late Jim Quick in his book on nymph fishing described two methods of fishing a deeply sunk fly. First, a 4-inch dropper is tied about 2½ to 3 feet above the nymph. Several split shots are attached to this. A simpler method is to place two or three split shots about the same distance up the leader. Now the fun begins! The experts speak knowingly of striking when there is a pause in the drift of the leader, or maintaining sufficient tension on the line to feel the strike.

Fishing a weighted nymph, to me, is akin to lure or bait fishing. I do it at times because I like to catch trout, but I do not get the sense of achievement from this method that I get when I fish a nymph fly with no weight.

What has held back nymph fishing from being as popular as other methods of fly fishing? For one thing, it is a difficult technique to master.

When the fly is much below a foot in depth, it is difficult to see or feel the trout strike. The freely drifting nymph is the most effective but in fast water there is a problem in sinking it to any depth. If the nymph is weighted enough to get it to the proper depth, it then loses its ability to float freely and naturally. Trout are more finicky about color, size, and shape in ideal nymph water than they are about dry and wet flies that are fished in the conventional manner.

With all the difficulties found in nymph and nymph fly fishing, I have never met a truly great fisherman who did not agree that the nymph fly and nymph, fished with a natural free drift, is the deadliest method for catching trout. When sufficient fishermen learn to use the nymph properly, our streams could really become fished-out. There is one satisfaction: by the time a fisherman gains these skills, he has long ago become a fish returner.

In the six years that have passed since the publication of the first edition of *The Art & Science of Fly Fishing*, I have spent most of my time fishing for trout with a nymph. I have arrived at certain conclusions that differ from many of the ideas of the late Jim Quick, author of the classic American book on nymph fishing.

One afternoon, after work, I was discussing nymph fly fishing with one of America's most popular fishing writers and author of a book on this subject. We will call this gentleman George. George is a master of the nymph fly in slow-moving Eastern streams, continuing the tradition of the founder of nymph fishing, G. E. M. Skues.

"George," I said, "in the past year I have been having much greater success with nymphs and nymph flies than ever before. In such rivers like Deschutes, with deep fast riffles that have lots of rocks in them, most of the time the nymph must be fished down deep next to the bottom. Jim Quick put his split shot about two and a half feet up the leader from the end fly. I get my best results if I clamp on one split shot six or eight inches above the fly, never directly next to the head of the fly. A split shot next to the head robs the fly of the flutter that is so necessary as it returns to you after a direct upstream cast.

Then came the explosion. George suddenly pushed his chair back, and grabbed each arm so tightly that his knuckles turned white. As he leaned toward me, his face became a purplish red, his eyes appeared to pop out. "Split shot, SPLIT SHOT! My God!"

As a physician, I recognized the beginning signs of apoplexy. At first I thought he was going to charge. Then, with monumental self-control, he composed himself, pulled his chair up to the table, and said, "Lenox, when is someone going to write up the techniques of lake nymph fishing that Cal Jordan has perfected? He won't do it. He has made a valuable contribution to fly fishing."

"George, I cannot tell you how bad I feel that I have offended you so deeply. I hope you will permit me to ask one question. Do you ever tie a little weight into your nymph flies?"

George became slightly pale, and he whispered across the table, "Just a very little lead wire." There was a long pause.

Moral: Do not ever discuss split shot and nymphs in "proper" fly fishing circles. But, if you want to catch trout feeding on nymphs at the bottom of a stream—and that's where they are most of the time—in my opinion you'd do well to use split shot.

Before we move on downstream, here are a few more tricks for fishing a nymph either with or without splitshot. When a cast is made directly upstream, the retrieve of the line must be as fast or even faster than with a dry fly. With this presentation, the fish usually takes the nymph going upstream. It is often possible to feel the strike.

When the quartering upstream presentation is used, the nymph usually sinks as it drifts naturally downstream. It is difficult to tell when the fish strikes. The angler must observe the knot between the leader and line or the dropper dry fly. At the very moment that there is a visible pause, he must strike. Sometimes, instead of a pause, there will be a sudden movement of the line, called by Skues "the draw." This, too, can only be seen by careful observation of the leader knot or the dropper dry fly.

Another big problem occurs when both leader knot and dropper dry fly are under water and not visible. Then it is almost impossible to see either the pause in line movement or the draw. It is possible to get around this problem by painting a small red circle on the line about every four feet for a distance of about twelve feet. Then when the knot or dropper fly are not visible, any change in movement can be ascertained by watching one of the red rings.

We have talked long enough. Let's walk down to the Undercut Bank Pool.

UNDERCUT BANKS

This section of stream consists of a long stretch of water in a large river. On the left, 100 yards upriver, there is an island. Behind us the river continues on a straight downstream course for approximately 20 yards, where it gradually shallows to about 6 inches.

The factor that makes this section a terrific fish producer is the undercut bank (see Plate 10, Fig. 24). The undercut varies in depth by 1 to 2 feet. The river flow is relatively fast and the bottom is rocky. Where we are standing the depth of the water is about 4 feet.

How are we going to fish this?

The best method is either to wade out from the opposite bank, as we did in the last pool, or fish it from a boat about 50 feet from the shore. However, the river is about 6 feet deep in this region and, fortunately for the river, no boat fishing is allowed. Standing on the bank and fishing upstream will work, but it necessitates a cast over the left shoulder. Silhouetted against the sky, you are visible to the trout for a radius of 20 to 30 feet. This visibility cuts down on the amount of fishable water. One satisfactory method of fishing this is by wading.

Fig. 24. Undercut bank.

CROSS SECTION

Plate 10.

First, we will try a dry fly. Start fishing directly upstream. From this location place your fly as close to the bank as possible and then work it out from the edge gradually. Keep your eyes open, as the fish will many times swim out from the bank and feed on natural flies toward the middle. If the dry fly does not work, try fishing a nymph fly upstream.

You have now worked your way upstream about 100 yards and have been fortunate enough to catch and release several nice fish. What a beautiful day, and what a nice stretch of stream. Now is a good time to fish another stretch of water for about a half an hour, allowing this area to rest; we will then come back here and fish downstream with a sunken streamer fly.

The half hour has passed, and we are ready to go at it again. The average fisherman who attempts to wade this will simply wade downstream and the result will be no fish. The proper method is as follows:

You should approach the bank from at least 25 yards away, and walk directly in as gently as possible. Step quietly into the water, don't fish . . . just stand absolutely still for five minutes or more. Then false-cast about 15 feet of line. Work out the remainder of the needed line. At first, work about 20 feet of line out and bring it back with little jerks. Next, cast quartering from the bank until you have worked the middle section of the stream. Now let out more line and repeat the process. After you have fished over about 50 feet of the stream, you will be ready to go downstream. Do not wade! Climb out on the bank and walk back 50 feet from the river's edge. Go downstream about two thirds of the distance that your line and fly previously covered, then walk directly in and repeat the process of waiting and then fishing. In this manner the fish will not hear and feel the vibrations of your walking.

You can also use this same S curve method with a long line and fish a dry fly without drag downstream.

CHAPTER ELEVEN

Middle of July

MIDDAY FISHING

THE TIME IS THE middle of July, and we are camped along a lovely river. Because we arrived at camp in the small hours of the morning, we both agreed to sleep late. By the time we have had breakfast and finished our camp chores, it is about 10:30 in the morning. Consequently, we will do most of our fishing in the midday period. Actually, I prefer this time because most of the other fishermen have retired from the river.

There is no accounting for fly hatches or fish feeding periods. During the summer months there is usually a hatch sometime during the day, most often between 10 A.M. and 2 P.M.

There is a secret to midday fishing during the summer. It can be summed up in one word, *shade*. Trout seek the shade for two reasons. They are less visible to their enemies and they frequently find food under the shade of trees. Even if the awaited midday hatch does not come off, some caddis, stoneflies, and mayflies that have been hatched at a previous time

Fig. 25. Midday water.

collect under the leaves and branches of shade trees during
the warm, sunny periods of the day. At times, they become
active and frequently fall or fly down to the water. The trout
are aware of this, and will wait under the shade trees for this
bounty of food. This phenomenon may occur during the middle of the day on dull, overcast days.

Let's go up to Hinton's Flat and look at the river. Now
look at Plates 11 and 12, Fig. 25. This is midday water. Notice
the patches of shade under the trees and grass clumps. There
goes an olive dun off the water! There goes another! There
. . . a good fish just rose! What are we waiting for?

Use a short line and a side-arm cast to put your fly up under
those trees. You are going to have to wade upstream and
crouch under the trees to do it.

If the hatch under those trees peters out, don't spend a great

Plate 11.

Plate 12.

deal of time fishing that water . . . keep moving! During the midday period a stretch of water may be completely dead, while around the bend great activity may be taking place.

In contrast, at dusk the best procedure is to pick a likely stretch of water and stay with it. The best period of dusk-fishing usually lasts only half an hour and you may miss it going from place to place.

Remember, though, for midday fishing, the thing to do is to keep moving!

DAPPING

On your way back upstream, stop at that pocket I showed you earlier in the day (Plate 12, Fig. 25). That is a marvelous spot for dapping. What do I mean by dapping? That's the same as piddle-fishing! You kind of piddle your fly in the water. Clear, isn't it?

Dapping is an old English term that goes back to the roots of fly fishing. I believe Isaak Walton and Charles Cotten spoke of dapping.

You sneak up to within about 6 or 8 feet of the bank, extend your rod out over the bank with just enough line so that your fly will land on the water, float a foot or so—then quietly lift it off the water and repeat the process.

In the spot shown on Plate 12, Fig. 25, kneel or even lie on your belly about 4 or 5 feet back from the bank, parallel to the bush with the flowers. Extend your rod tip out and drop your fly right next to those yellow flowers, then gradually extend your fly until it floats in the white water. When you have fished that out, walk downstream about 30 feet, slide into the water, and cast your fly up against the lower side of the clump of grass just above the bush with the flowers. I saw a large trout rise there last night. I am sure he is still there.

Another spot that is ideal for dapping is shown in Plate 11, Fig. 25. Instead of wading up under those trees and casting to that big rock, tiptoe out to a point 6 feet from the bank and dapp your fly right behind it. This is the only way that you can fish some brushy spots.

MOSS BANK HOLE

We have finished dapping. Darkness is upon us, and we are walking to camp.

You asked me earlier in the day about chalk streams and whether we have them in this country. Chalk streams are found in England. They are typically slow, meandering streams that flow through and out of chalk deposits. The water is a very clear, at times they are literally choked with vegetation. They support a tremendous amount of insect life. The English differentiate between chalk and limestone streams. The actual difference between these streams is more geologic, the water being similar in both. What makes these streams such tremendous fish producers is the hardness, or lime content, of the water. The hardness of the water determines the amount of insect life that can thrive in a stream and, thus, the number of fish it will support. In his book *How to Fish from Top to Bottom*, Sid Gordon explains this in great detail and gives simple methods of chemical analysis for the lime content of water.

For years American fishing writers denied the existence of chalk or limestone streams in this country. They were wrong. There are not any true chalk streams, but typical limestone streams do exist in parts of the Middle West and Pennsylvania. The Letort in Pennsylvania is a limestone stream even though it looks like a typical chalk stream. I am told that if one were to blindfold the late Skues, father of the modern nymph, and drop him on the Letort, he would think he was still fishing one of his own beloved English chalk streams. Charles Fox's book *This Wonderful World of Trout* describes this stream in full detail.

I have never knowingly fished a true limestone stream. Silver Creek, a hard-water stream in Idaho, comes close to fitting this description. The river we will fish tomorrow is classified as semi-hard water. In a few spots it presents some of the typical aspects of very-hard water.

Morning is upon us, and we have driven over to the moss bank hole. The word "moss" is bandied about loosely by fishermen. The so-called "moss bed" you see in Plate 13, Fig. 26,

CROSS SECTION

Fig. 26. Moss bed pool.

Plate 13.

is not moss at all but is made up of true aquatic plants, commonly called water weeds. These particular weeds provide an excellent nursery for aquatic insects, snails, plankton, shrimp, etc.

When I took this picture, the river was high enough to completely cover the moss or weed bed. Look carefully at the plate and you will notice an irregular coloration extending out from the shore into the river. This is the moss, or weed bed. Later in the season the tips of the weeds will be visible. Trout like to lie up against these weeds.

When you fish this hole, cast upstream and place your fly at the edge of the moss bank. The water is too deep to wade at the outer edge of the moss bed, so you must wade up through the moss. You must wade carefully. The velocity of the water is slow in amongst the weeds, and trout will be able to hear you for a long distance both up- and downstream. It can be waded downstream by the method described in the undercut-bank section of this book (page 48).

Aquatic plants are not always desirable in a stream. It is possible to introduce the wrong plants into a stream and ruin it by actually choking up the stream. Even in some of the best chalk and limestone streams in England, the proper plants become too thick, and they must be thinned out at certain times of the year in order to maintain good fishing.

Every four or five years the moss beds in Silver Creek, Idaho, wash out and with them go the fish . . . much to the consternation of the fishermen. I wonder if this is not Nature's way of keeping this stream in a healthy state?

I can see you are impatient to start fishing this stretch. Good luck, and wade slowly and carefully. Don't get discouraged if most of the fish run into the weeds and break you off.

MUDDY WATER

This morning, fishing conditions are not very auspicious. A sudden rain last night sent the stream up about 6 inches. The water is muddy, about the color of coffee. But this situation is not as bad as it first appears. If you will look carefully at the bank, you will notice that the water has fallen about an inch.

This is a beautiful, sunny, middle-of-June day, the time of the largest mayfly hatches for these streams. The sun is just beginning to warm the water, and already a few red uprights can be seen. In the past I have had fine fishing in just this situation . . . falling water, plus a large fly hatch, usually produces fine dry-fly fishing, no matter what the color of the water. If a white china plate is visible 2 feet beneath the surface, good fly-fishing is possible. The murkier the water, the more thoroughly one must fish any given stretch. Trout in crystal-clear water can see a fly within a radius of 20 to 30 feet; in very muddy water they must be within 6 inches of it and close to the surface. Hence, we must lengthen our casts 6 to 12 inches with each successive cast to fully cover the water.

Paradoxically, this is also true in very cold (40-to-45-degree), clear water when trout are at the bottom. In this type of water they can see the fly, but they are so sluggish that they will not bother to swim more than a few inches. This is particularly true of winter steelhead.

Let us suppose there are no obvious flies visible on the water, no trout rising, and the water is coffee-colored. What then? Bait is a logical choice, but I simply have no fun catching trout on bait. This is a situation for a large streamer fly; a #6 or even, at times, a #4. I use my old friend, the Bucktail Royal Coachman, a large streamer fly with a maribou wing. If this does not work, then a fluorescent fly will often turn the trick. I don't consider this a true fly . . . but a lure. It may be necessary to place a split shot ahead of the fly or use a weighted fly. A quartering downstream cast is used. Fish the usual areas where one would expect to find trout, but also fish the quiet regions where you would not usually bother. Mr. Hewitt, in his classic book *Telling on the Trout,* writes of catching trout in the grass of the meadows that border the Neversink River at flood stages. They also seem to like the tail-end of pools at this time.

Well, a good two hours have passed. The water is still falling. Let's get on with our fishing.

I have saved one of my favorite spots for our trip today. This will be a short trip and we will spend only a few hours fishing the island (Plate 14, Fig. 27). The largest fish I have caught have been around islands. We will wade out to this island; check your life preserver!

Where do you want to start fishing? The water on the left, looking upstream, is excellent, especially behind the rocks near the large tree. The shadow from that large tree will provide ample shade. This picture was taken about 4 o'clock in the afternoon on a mid-summer day. Shadows are present on the water just at the edge of the rocks. On the right side of the island is a typical riffle with the characteristic meeting of fast and slow water. Your comments on how to fish this are correct, however, you have missed the best location for big fish . . . the tail-end of the island. An island is nothing but a big rock. More trout hold behind a rock than at the sides or at the front. Examine Figure 27 . . . carefully! Where the two currents come together downstream is the hot spot for big trout. Unfortunately, this is not shown in the picture, and you must rely on the drawing. The biggest trout I have ever caught have been in this location.

First, cast a dry fly downstream with big S curves in the line about 3 feet above the hot spot, and allow your fly to drift down until drag develops. I particularly like to fish this spot with a dry fly and a sinking line. By the time the fly starts to drag, the line has sunk down quite a good distance. Then, bring it back with little jerks as a sunken wet fly. When the fly is in the region of the hot spot, allow it to hang for a few

Fig. 27. Island.

Plate 14.

minutes. Some anglers keep their fly in this location for as long as five or ten minutes before finally bringing it in.

You fish this area and I will commence fishing on the left side of the island and work my way upstream. You should spend at least a half-hour working the tail of the island. When you have finished this, then fish that riffle to the right.

Fishing Adages

GOOD FISHING

1. Rising barometer.
2. Falling water.
3. Dark of the moon.

POOR FISHING

1. East wind.
2. Falling barometer.
3. Rising water.
4. First bright day after several dark or rainy days (or vice versa).
5. Full moon.
6. Thunder.

PART III

Salmon, Steelhead, and Others

CHAPTER TWELVE

Anadromous Salmon and Trout of the Pacific Coast

NATIVE TO THE Pacific Coast of North America are two species of anadromous (seagoing) trout, steelhead (rainbow) and cutthroat (harvest), belonging to the genus *Salmo*. In this same genus are the Atlantic salmon and sea trout (brown) of the Atlantic coast. There are five species of salmon that inhabit the rivers of the Pacific Coast: chinook, silver, pink, chum, and sockeye. They belong to the genus *Oncorhynchus*. All of the salmon of the genus *Oncorhynchus* die after spawning, while those of the genus *Salmo* do not. Three of these fish are of interest to the fly-fisherman on the West coast. Supreme above all is the steelhead *(Salmo gairdneri),* followed in relative importance by the cutthroat *(Salmo clarki)* and the silver salmon *(Oncorhynchus kisuth).* The chinook salmon will occasionally take a fly, but the pink, chum, and sockeye seldom will. The steelhead and cutthroat take a fly best in fresh water, while the silver takes best in salt water. Only in certain streams in Canada is the silver salmon truly a first-class fresh-water fly

129

fish. The steelhead and cutthroat are the only varieties that have subspecies that remain in fresh water all of their lives.

In the Pacific Northwest the resident rainbow and the steelhead are often found in the same stream. Why the rainbow remains all of its life in fresh water and the steelhead goes to sea has never been explained. The steelhead fresh from the sea is a beautiful steely-gray color. Then as it approaches the spawning period, it takes on the coloration of the nonmigratory rainbow. The cutthroat returning from the sea is a bluish gray, becoming darker and more spotted as it approaches the reproductive period. The silver salmon loses its bright silver color and becomes very dark just before spawning. The males of all of the species develop a hooked jaw just before their reproductive period. The young silvers take about a year to work their way down the river into the ocean, where they spend anywhere from one to five years maturing. Finally, the mature fish ascends the river to repeat the cycle. Only about 20 percent of the average steelhead run—but most of the cutthroat—manage to return to the sea after spawning.

The two species of anadromous *Salmonidae* of the East Coast, Atlantic salmon and brown trout, are of utmost interest to steelhead fishermen of the Pacific Coast. Experts who have fished for steelhead and Atlantic salmon state that the two are fished for in a surprisingly similar manner. They emphasize that both fish behave in rivers in almost identical fashion. Jack Hemingway, son of Ernest Hemingway, proved this to me by coming directly from the Atlantic salmon streams and successfully catching steelhead on a fly. Spencer Biddle journeyed to Norway and had no difficulty catching Atlantic salmon and sea trout (brown trout) with his West Coast flies.

Our present-day steelhead fly-fishing techniques were developed on the Atlantic salmon streams. Every time I think a new technique has been developed on the Pacific Coast, I find the same method mentioned in some old English fishing book. Proof of the magnitude of the English contribution can be found in *Salmon Fishing*,* an encyclopedia of Atlantic salmon fishing edited by the late Eric Tavner.

American fly-fishermen have, however, contributed enormously to streamlining the sport. They have popularized the use of light rods, 6-foot, 1¾-ounce midge rods, 9-foot, 5-ounce standard rods. Many large salmon, twelve pounds to twenty pounds, are landed every year with relative ease on these small midge rods. One of our biggest contributions to the sport has been the development and perfection of fly lines made of synthetic fibers and various plastic coatings. There are a few diehard anglers on both sides of the Atlantic who still use the old English silk lines, but it is difficult to obtain them even in England.

It is in the field of casting that the United States anglers have made their biggest contribution. The use of ultra light tackle has been made possible by the double-haul method of casting, wherein the line is pulled as the fisherman makes his false cast. It increases the average caster's distance by a third to a half.

Each year more and more people fish for steelhead. The West Coast is blessed with many rivers. However, the sport has been able to maintain itself only through intensive federal and state stocking programs. Ultimately, most of the spring and summer run fish will have to be returned to the river in order to maintain these runs and still provide adequate sport for the masses of fishermen. The most sporting and enjoyable method of catching a steelhead is with a fly.

*This book was published by J. B. Lippincott in this country during the late 1930s and is still in print in England. Hardy Bros. in London, England can obtain a copy. Every serious student of the sport of fly fishing should read his book *Trout Fishing from All Angles,* as well as his encyclopedia. They are big books and, like so many of the older English sporting books, dull and ponderous with too much attention paid to unimportant minutiae. They should prove to the reader that we Americans may polish and perfect methods of angling but it is doubtful that we will invent any new techniques of fly presentation.

CHAPTER THIRTEEN

Tackle and Casting

THE BASIC 8½-FOOT, 4-ounce parabolic-action rod discussed in Chapter 1 (page 19) will do well for most steelhead fishing with casts up to 70 feet. Unless you can cast that far, you might as well stay home—steelhead fly fishing and long casting go hand in hand. For very long casts over 70 feet, I prefer a heavier (5-ounce) and stiffer 8½- or 9-foot parabolic-action rod. There is only one reason for long rods—long casts. A short 2-ounce rod can land a steelhead just as well as a long one. If you are a Lee Wulff, you may be able to cast 90 feet with a 6-foot midge rod, but if you are like this writer, you will need everything going for you, so stick to the long rod.

FLY LINES

The basic sinking line described in Chapter I (page 21) will suffice for steelhead fishing, but I prefer a wet tip or wet-head forward-tapered line. This line has a high-density sinking tip, with the remainder of the line being of the floating type. The floating line allows for easy mending, while the weight-forward design adds distance to the cast. While a forward-tapered line does not mend as well as a double-tapered one, it will mend adequately for most steelhead fly-fishing. A hundred yards of backing is an absolute necessity in steelhead fishing.

LEADERS

Leaders present somewhat of a dilemma. During high water a 9-foot, 10-pound leader is adequate. During average clear water conditions an 8-pound leader does well. But in very low water some anglers go down to 4-pound test. Stop and imagine fishing all day and then hooking a 12-pound steelhead on a 4-pound leader. This problem usually resolves itself in favor of the fish. Consequently, most of the time 6-pound test is the lightest practical test.

Level leaders in the 10- and 8-pound sizes are considered the best by many experienced anglers. They turn over at the end of a cast almost as well as the tapered variety and are far less visible. A tapered leader in the heavier sizes has a very heavy and visible butt section. From 6-pound test down, the tapered leader is a necessity.

During the late spring until the winter months I use a dropper fly about two to three feet up from the tip of the leader. However, when the fly must be fished deep the dropper is not used. It tends to keep the leader from sinking.

THE DOUBLE-HAUL

A fly fisherman who cannot cast at least seventy feet consistently with ease will catch few steelhead. Seventy feet is a stumbling block for most novice casters. There is no problem in casting thirty or forty feet with the sloppiest technique; after that the problems develop. There is one single casting exercise that will correct most faults. *As your back-cast passes your head, look behind. If your back-cast is not high, the next time make it go high and you will automatically correct your casting fault.* This is the secret of the high line fly casting developed by the Austrians on Alpine trout streams and popularized by Charles Ritz.

The average good caster using conventional casting techniques can seldom cast much further than eighty feet. How many times one hears a fellow fly fisherman discuss casting— "I had to cast one hundred feet to reach him. He weighed five pounds!" Long casts, like mammoth fish, grow with the telling.

However, if the angler has mastered the Double-Haul, casts of one hundred feet under actual fishing conditions are not unusual.

At times there appears in the fly fishing literature a classic description of a technique. Such is the monograph entitled, "To Cast a Fly," published by Scientific Anglers.

The following is a direct quote from the section entitled "More Distance." After reading this you may desire to go back over the basic fundamentals of casting expressed in a different manner than in this book. Write to your favorite fly fishing shop and request a copy. Price 50¢.

MORE DISTANCE

The double haul is not hard to perform, but it is difficult to describe. It is a casting method that produces a tremendous increase in the line velocity during the forward and back cast. This increase in speed of the line allows more line to be in the air by false casting and allows a much longer line shoot.

Before you learn the double haul you must master the first step, the single haul. Many anglers only use this technique to obtain more distance. Once you have learned the single haul, however, the transition to the double haul is easy.

Start casting in the usual manner. On the back cast, at the instant the rod is stopped at 1:00 o'clock, give a hard, two-foot pull on the line with your left hand, thus adding velocity to the back cast. The increased velocity of the back cast produced by the pull, or haul, will enable more line to shoot out with the forward cast. Let your left hand drift up to the first guide of the rod just before the rod reaches the 1:00 o'clock position. The haul will be easier to perform. Practice the single haul under actual fishing conditions before going on to the next step.

Then, after it has become comfortable and you are able to increase your casting distance, it is time to learn the double haul.

In regular casting the forward cast is stopped at 11:00 o'clock. In the second stage of the double haul the rod is stopped at 11:00 o'clock, and a second pull is given with the left hand, thus increasing the velocity of the line even more.

When you reach the 11:00 o'clock position and give the second pull with your left hand, then if you desire to shoot the line and complete the cast, release the line in your left hand, but do not stop the rod. Deliberately bring the rod tip forward until the rod is almost parallel to the water. Unless you bring the rod almost parallel to the water, the fly will catch in the leader as it turns over at the end of the cast. Failure to master this one simple final maneuver kept me from doing satisfactory double hauls for many years. It was not until Mike Kennedy showed me this simple trick that I could perform a reasonable double haul.

Once the rhythm of the double haul is learned, it is a glorious sensation. Recently, my guide and boatman, one of Prince Helfrich's sons, turned to me, "Doc, the Rogue isn't that big, you're overcasting the water." The young whippersnapper was right; I was enjoying double hauling so much that I was making my cast too long.

The double haul is particularly useful for casting into the wind and casting a weighted fly. Be sure and wear protective glasses with that weighted fly.

In the past few years two, inexpensive, short pamphlets have been published—'To Cast a Fly,' by Scientific Anglers, and 'Fly Casting,' written by Jim Green and published by the Fenwick Rod Company. These books both explain fly casting better than anything I have written in this book. I strongly advise you to get both of them. Each describes different little tricks in casting. Most fly-fishing shops carry them.

CHAPTER FOURTEEN

Location and Lies of Steelhead

LOCATION

IN TROUT FISHING the angler merely has to read water to find trout. In anadromous fishing he must find their location on any particular day during the run. Steelhead tend to run in waves. One day there will be lots of fish in one area and the next day it will be empty. When they are running fast they may cover ten miles in one day. If you are not casting over fish, you will not catch any—simple, isn't it?

In the old days steelhead fishermen had only to contend with naturally spawned steelhead. In the past fifteen years there has been an increasing emphasis on stocking artificially spawned and hatchery raised steelhead smolts. These fish have a much different migration pattern than the wild variety. Before going into a discussion of a stocked steelhead migration, it is more appropriate to discuss the wild fish.

The speed with which a wild fish travels depends on how close he is to spawning. Winter fish are usually about a month or two away from spawning. Consequently they rush right up to their home pools. Spring and summer steelhead run very slowly up their rivers. An April fish may take three or more months to reach its home pool. They may be six or seven months from spawning.

These fish are so strong and full of fight that they have broken my leader going upstream after a forty-five-minute contest. However, it is common to land a winter fish in five or ten minutes. This is the reason seasoned steelhead fishermen prefer to fish in spring and summer, while the meat fisherman loves winter. The winter runs are larger and the fish easier to catch on bait and the more difficult on a fly.

Steelhead fresh from the ocean will take a fly much more readily than fish that have been residing in a pool for a long period of time. Under optimum circumstances, fresh arrivals in home pools may take a fly readily for periods of hours at a time. Fish that have been in a pool for weeks or months may take a fly, very carefully fished, for only a five minute period or not at all during the course of days.

A. E. Wood made the statement, "Atlantic salmon that travel long distances against difficult rapids do not fight well until rested." A recent experience of mine seems to bear this out.

A long distance up the Columbia, another river flows into it that has a fine August run of summer steelhead. I arrived at the mouth one summer day and was informed by the other fishermen that a fresh run was going into the river. That evening just before dark I hooked a bright 6-pound female. I was astounded, it took me about ten minutes to land her. At this time of year in the rivers emptying into the lower Columbia, a fresh steelhead would have taken at least thirty minutes to land.

One other explanation for this phenomenon is nitrogen disease. There are so many dams on the Columbia that during high water the turbulent flow of water over the dam spillways literally beats nitrogen and oxygen into the water. The oxygen is rapidly eliminated from the water but not the nitrogen. After the water has passed over five or six dams the nitrogen content becomes dangerous for fish. These fish die of a condition similar to the bends suffered by divers. Consequently in May and June, when the Columbia is in flood stage, large numbers of both upstream and downstream migrants die of this disease.

On and on we go, polluting and destroying our natural resources. Let us go back to the more pleasant discussion of migrating steelhead.

On certain rivers, in the fall, after they have been in their home pools for a prolonged time, fish will start to take a dry fly avidly. Rarely will they do this unless there is an actual hatch of large caddis or stoneflies.

One late October day in 1949, I watched about a dozen steelhead rising to numerous large red-brown caddis. They were eagerly feeding and I hooked about five of them. Sad to say, I killed two. I shall always look back on this day as one of infamy in my career as a fly fisherman. Today the game commission rightly protects these pools. These fish fought poorly and, although still some two months from spawning, they had been in their home pool for about four to six months. Consequently their energy reserves were at a low ebb and they were simply unable to fight with any vigor.

When a salmon or trout first hatches from the egg, it is called fry. When they are about 2-4 inches in length they have distinctive cross bars on their sides. When they reach the length of six or seven inches they lose the cross bars (parr marks). They are bright and silvery in appearance and are referred to as smolts. At this time they start migrating to the sea. A 7-inch steelhead smolt and a 7-inch resident trout look like entirely different fish. Unfortunately, uninformed anglers catch hundreds of smolts each year, calling them trout. On many streams the fish and game commission have raised the legal limit to ten inches at certain times of the year to protect smolts.

Steelheads stocked as smolts are an entirely different problem compared to the native wild variety. To express it in one sentence: they act like late winter fish no matter what season they are running up a stream. Although it has been possible to stock steelhead smolts for some time, only recently have fish biologists been successful in having them return as spring or summer fish. Prior to this they always came back as winter fish. The time of year and size at release are the crucial determining factors that make these immature fish return at the right time. But alas when they do return, they rush upstream in a big wave until they reach the release spot. For this reason the release spot is usually located in protected water. Unless the fisherman is on the river at the time the fish are running, he is out of luck. Consequently, the man who can hurry to a stream after a storm at the opportune moment when the water is falling and clearing will catch steelhead. The working or tourist angler who must plan his fishing for a certain day, may return fishless. When stocked fish are running, keep moving over as much territory as possible until the run is located. Anadromous fish that are traveling can cover ten miles a day, hence they can be in the release spot in most streams in three or four days or less.

Many times an angler correctly locates the position of the run but still is unable to catch fish simply because of competition from bait and spin fishermen. There is only one way to win: cover water that they cannot or will not fish. Many steelhead rivers have roads paralleling them. When the run is on, from the dawn's break to dark, hordes of bait fishermen pound every hole and riffle. However, most of these anglers only fish the road side of the river. By crossing to the other side of the river the fly fisherman can fish water that is untouched. This is the reason a small rubber boat is as important a piece of equipment as are waders.

If the bait fisherman can reach the riffle, do not fish it.

STEELHEAD LIES

In the chapter on "Reading Water," a typical pool was described as having a riffle or rapid at its head, a center with slow moving deep water and the tail end with a shelving bottom that gradually shallows until it forms a lip or break. As a rule steelhead are found toward the head and tail of a pool. In the late fall, winter, and early spring when the water is high and cold they will be found more toward the middle. By the end of spring, during summer, and early fall the water is usually clear, low, and warm. Then they lie in the upper and lower ends of a pool. Here the water is shallow, fast, and broken. The main reason for this low water position is oxygen. The warmer the water the less oxygen. Turbulence in water increases the oxygen. Many times I have observed steelhead holding in such rapid water that I could not believe it possible for a fish to maintain a position without constantly swimming. Yet there they were apparently motionless. The answer is rocks. Steelhead love rocks and the pockets they form. They are seldom found in sandy areas.

RUNS

Many times you will hear fishermen speak of fishing runs. These are distinct channels in a stream that steelhead, salmon and cutthroat travel when they are migrating. During shallow water stages it is possible to visualize these runs. Then, when there has been a slight rise in the water level due to rain, it is possible to actually observe fish passing through these runs. This is a logical place to present a fly, especially when the water is dropping, clearing, and the steelhead are moving on up the river. It is at this point that the steelhead may differ from the Atlantic salmon. British Atlantic salmon experts claim that salmon seldom take a fly when traveling (passage fish). They only begin to take when they stop for a temporary rest. My experience has been that traveling steelhead take a fly readily, providing the angler knows the runs.

HOLDING AND FEEDING WATER

The steelhead's home pool is also referred to as "holding water." Here they rest for prolonged periods before continuing their migration or until they spawn. When you find such a pool, look upstream for "feeding water." This is usually a riffle full of large rocks. The riffle may be fifty feet or a hundred yards above the holding water. Steelhead go back and forth between holding and feeding water during the course of the day. At dawn and dusk summer fish are likely to be in the feeding areas. They take a fly most readily in this water. However, do not neglect the middle of the day. Spencer Biddle claimed he caught more fish at noon than at any other time.

LEDGES

Look for rocky ledges; steelhead frequently lie close to these. They are best fished from the opposite side of the stream.

Holding water also contains feeding or striking fish. The terms holding and feeding may only be an exercise in semantics. The fact to remember is: at certain times steelhead are found in fast riffles and at other times in obvious pools. They are commonly found in both locations at the same time. When fishing a pool, concentrate on the fast head and tail in summer and the slower middle areas in winter. In certain rivers more steelhead are caught in the upper part of the pool, while in others such as the Rogue River, they are caught in the tail. Part of the explanation for this phenomenon may be shelter. Tail ends of pools in the Rogue are apt to be deep with larger rocks scattered about, while tail ends of pools in other steelhead rivers tend to be shallow without protection. At dusk, however, these shallow tail ends often contain fish.

In summer low water the steelhead tend to lie in shallow rough water. But let there be a sudden freshet with an abrupt rise caused by colder water and they will take up locations in deeper smoother water.

During the winter flooding steelhead frequenty lie close to the banks. Under such conditions I have often had steelhead take a lure right next to the bank.

Every river has high water lies and low water lies. Although an experienced angler may figure these out, there is no substitute for local knowledge. This is the reason for fishing gillies (guides) on English salmon rivers. Unfortunately I know of no guides for wading fly-fishermen in the U.S.A. All of our licensed guides are boat guides. Most guides will not allow their anglers to wade. Often wading is the most effective way to catch steelhead.

CHAPTER FIFTEEN

Steelhead Flies

THERE IS NO FORM of fly fishing that requires a greater knowledge of the river, and ability to read water, than fly fishing for steelhead, with the exception of the Atlantic salmon. The greatest feat any angler can perform today is to catch one of these fish in public water on a fly. I will make one exception to this statement—the Rogue River, with such boating guides as Prince Helfrich and his sons, Ed Thurston, the Prewitt boys and other professional guides. Here the guides are important. A twelve-year-old boy who has never seen a fly rod can catch steelhead on a fly when such a guide is maneuvering the boat.

The fisherman who can catch a steelhead on the West Coast and an Atlantic salmon on the East Coast in public water with any degree of regularity is a master fly-fisherman. I wonder how well those East Coast anglers who fish the private club waters of the Miramichi and other New Brunswick rivers with such fabulous results would do on the North Fork of the Stillaquamish. This river is about an hour's drive from Seattle.

143

The best part is closed for fly fishing only. On weekends the anglers line up elbow to elbow and gradually walk down the bank. When one reaches the end of the pool he then walks to the head of the line and starts over.

One weekend on the Stillaquamish I watched Spencer Biddle catch two steelhead. There was only one other fish caught. At least twenty-five fly fishermen, including myself, lined up with him casting in the same pool, when he performed this feat.

The only other steelhead was caught by a lady angler. This lady did not play her fish with the reel but ran back and forth up and down the bank shrieking at the top of her lungs; much to the assembled multitude's amusement.

It was not just luck that made Mr. Biddle outfish the hordes of fishermen that weekend. It was his superb knowledge of fly presentation that turned the trick.

Fly Presentation

The oldest technique of presenting a fly has been humorously called by our English cousins, "Chuck and Chance it." It is still the most commonly used technique. On page 32 the paragraph entitled "Quartering Down and Across" is the description of the Chuck and Chance It method. Please go back and read this paragraph.

It's called Chuck and Chance It because the angler simply chucks the fly quartering downstream and it's considered by chance that the steelhead will strike the fly. Actually when this technique is done properly, it is not just by chance that the fish strikes. A secret of successful Chuck and Chance It fly presentation is to fish all of the water close to the angler as well as the distant shore. Another secret is to put enough mends in the line to keep that fly swimming slowly broadside to the current, down to the waiting steelhead.

Frank Moore, proprietor of the fishing lodge at Steamboat on the North Umpaqua River, is a master of this technique. He uses many small mends and is able to fish a surprisingly tight line. Yet he keeps the fly broadside to the current.

After the fisherman has worked all the water in front of him he then walks down the stream about one third of his maximum cast and starts over.

In 1903 a revolutionary technique for fly-fishing for salmon was discovered by A. H. E. Wood. He wrote of this technique and its discovery in the previously mentioned encyclopedia *Salmon Fishing*. It is very interesting to go back through the years to 1903 and read how he discovered and perfected this technique.

Greased-Line Fishing

by A. H. E. Wood

1. *The birth of the idea.*

One afternoon in July 1903 I was fishing an Irish river. The weather for some time past had been exceptionally hot and dry, so that the river had dropped considerably and was very clear. I had had no sport all day and sat down to think beside a pool full of salmon that had steadily refused to look at a series of flies, presented to them, as I thought, in every possible way. Shortly afterward, I saw one fish and then another rise to something floating down on the surface of the water. This continued at irregular intervals; and at length I was fortunately able to observe the cause, namely, a sort of white moth similar to those often seen amongst the heather.

I went to the head of the pool, which consisted of an eel-weir, and there found a number of salmon lying with their noses pushed right up to the sill. As luck had it, I happened to have with me a White Moth troutfly; this I tied on the cast and sat on the plank-bridge over the weir. Then holding the gut in my hand, I dibbled the fly over them. After some minutes, one of the salmon became curious enough to rise up to examine the fly, but at the last moment thought better of it; this I believe was due to its attention having been distracted by my feet, which were dangling over the plank, barely six feet away from the water. I changed my position, knelt on the bridge and let down the fly. This time the fish came more boldly at the fly and it was followed by others; but I had pricked several before I realized that, because I was kneeling directly above them, I was, in striking, pulling the hook straight out of their mouths. So I changed my tactics and, by letting go the cast at the right moment, succeeded in dropping the fly actually into the open mouth of the next fish that came up to it. I then picked up my rod, ran off the bridge, and made all haste downstream. All this time the line and cast were slack and floating down; yet when I tightened on the fish, I found it had hooked itself. By the use of this trick I landed six fish, lost others and pricked more than I care to say, all in a few hours. After that experience, I discovered myself fishing on the surface or as near to it as I was able. The final advance came, when I started using a greased line to assist in keeping the fly in the right position, and I thus evolved out of a simple experiment what has become a most interesting mode of salmon-angling, the greased-line method.

Further, my experience of greased-line fishing has shown me that a salmon is more ready to take a fly on or just under the surface than at any other level, except very near to the bottom. I therefore aim at keeping the fly at the surface, or sink it right down to the stones; and I have entirely forsaken the ordinary practice, which causes the fly to swim in mid-water.

A salmon is more ready to take a fly on or just under the surface than at any other level, except very near to the bottom. The same statement can be applied to steelhead.

The above statements are one of the true secrets of successful salmon and steelhead fishing.

Wood then went on to say that he always took two rods with him during the following periods of the year: spring, February, and March. One rod equipped with a floating line, the other with a heavy ungreased double-tapered line, the center made of 16 or 16½ S.W.G. (Standard Wire Gage). With this he fished a 1¾- to 2¾-inch Jack Scott fly, sunk as near to the bed of the river as he could get it, without catching the bottom. He used this method when, *the air is really colder than the water.*

The other rod was equipped with a greased double-tapered line. This was his surface greased line outfit. With this he fished a fly varying from 1¾ inches to one inch in length. On cold days and in the evening he fished the 1¾-inch fly, while during the middle of the day he used the one-inch or even smaller fly. Incidentally, with the one-inch or smaller he used a 1X gut leader. This is the equivalent of a nylon leader with a 6- to 8-pound tip.

The smaller the hook the more lightly he dressed the fly. He referred to these flies, size 4 to 10, as low water or light summer flies, *best when the water is clear.*

He then went on to describe greased line fishing as he finally evolved it, and as it is practiced throughout the world today.

Classic greased line fly fishing is the same as dry fly fishing with the fly sunk just under the surface. Most everything written in this book concerning the technique of presenting the fly without drag can be applied to greased line fishing. There is one factor that is more important in greased line fishing than in conventional dry fly fishing for trout, and that is the ability to mend. In dry fly fishing the angler fishes more upstream with a relatively short line, thirty to forty feet. In greased line much of the time the line is cast quartering up or quartering downstream with a line length of fifty to seventy feet. Hence to keep the fly from dragging frequent mends of different sizes are necessary when there are varying currents.

Wood emphasizes that, as much as possible, *the fly should be presented broadside to the fish.*

The time to use the greased line technique, *winter or summer* is when the air is warmer than the water.

There are other rather subtle differences: in dry fly fishing, the fly is cast so that there are initial curves in the line — either S curves or an upstream curve. The line is kept very slack. In greased line fly fishing the line is cast in a straight manner quartering up, directly across, or quartering downstream. At the first sign of drag a mend is placed in the line. The mend is only big enough to keep the fly from speeding up. In greased line fishing the fly is seldom cast directly upstream as it is in dry fishing.

Deep Sunk Fly Presentation

So far we have only discussed quartering downstream and greased line techniques with the fly just under the surface. During cold water conditions the fly must be sunk as deeply as possible.

The first discussion will pertain to the deep sunk technique using a high density rapid sinking line and a weighted fly. This technique is exactly the same as the previously described quartering downstream method, but be sure to wear safety glasses. A weighted fly with a heavy high density line is a dangerous weapon.

In the greased line deep technique the weight in the fly is utilized to get the fly down. Consequently the angler must cast at a much steeper angle upstream and utilize large mends to slow the fly and make it go deep. With this technique the fish usually hooks itself. All of a sudden the lucky angler finds himself playing a steelhead. The deep sunk fly is the best method to catch winter steelhead. If you are not frequently snagging your fly on the bottom you are not fishing deep enough.

Twitching the Fly

The greatest run of summer steelhead I ever saw in the Kalama River occurred in 1954. One day during the run Mr. Biddle and I were standing by one of his favorite pools. As we watched, a tremendous steelhead came completely out of the water. Mr. Biddle came to me and said, "Lenox, go catch him!"

I went after the fish slowly and carefully, casting in the usual manner, my fly three or four inches below the surface. Mr. Biddle stood and watched. Then, when I had gone through the pool, he started to fish. I sat on the bank and watched. Soon I realized he was fishing for this steelhead in an entirely different manner than I had ever seen him do before.

The day had been a warm one, dusk was approaching, and there was not a cloud in the sky. The water was clear, low and slow at this place. His greased line was floating; the fly was a fluffy Royal Coachman, number 8. He would cast it out and bring it back with little twitches across the top of the water, approaching nearer to the fish's position with each cast. Then, just downstream from where it had jumped, the steelhead rose completely out of the water and took the fly. Twenty-five minutes later he beached it, a beautiful 12-pounder.

There is another method of fly presentation that also uses the principal of controlled drag. The leader is tied in such a manner that it is tied to the hook just back of the eye and to the underside. This causes the head of the fly to ride high in the water. When it is retrieved it produces a large surface wake, thus attracting fish.

In Chapter 17, "A Steelhead Trip," we will put these various methods of fly presentation to use under actual stream conditions.

CHAPTER SIXTEEN

Flies

THE MORE EXPERT A fly fisherman becomes, the fewer the fly patterns he uses. Four or five patterns are enough for most steelhead, cutthroat and silver salmon fishing. I suspect the patterns that will be listed later in this chapter will do as well on eastern Atlantic salmon streams. The big factor is size. Hook sizes should vary from the very large #2 for high, cold water down to #8 or #10 for clear, low, warm water conditions.

Most flies used for anadromous fish are attractor patterns. However, in the past few years there has been a great deal of interest in the use of nymphs. The proportion of attractor to deceiver flies may change as we become more successful with this method.

Attractor flies should be covered by the following four basic color schemes:

A very bright pattern with a white wing, a black with a white wing, a brown with a brown wing, and finally a fluorescent fly with the color combination of yellow and red, for muddy water and winter fishing. This should be tied only on a #2 hook.

Nowhere in this book has any mention been made of fly weight. Greased line fishing calls for a standard weight hook. The fly must be just under the surface. But when water temperatures are 48 degrees or less, then the deep sunk fly is a must; this necessitates a weighted fly. Some anglers use a fly with extra weight tied into the shank of the hook, others like myself use varying sized split shot clamped to the leader at the head of the fly. There is no question that the split shot method tends to cause the fly to swim with a head down appearance. I vacillate between fine lead wire wound around the shank (before applying body material) and the split shot technique. With the split shot technique fewer flies are required which is a monetary saving.

Which fly, what size, and color? When asked, one old veteran growled, "Hell, when they're ready, steelhead will take any fly!" True—but they can also be enticed into striking.

Bright day, bright fly. Reasoning: the sun will cause the tinsel and bright colors to flash. On a dull day, use a dull fly for that reason. This rule reversed would probably catch as many fish. One of the reasons for using a dropper fly is to allow the use of combination of flies.

Size—this is even a bigger dilemma to most anglers. The following table should help as a rough guide.

SIZE OF FLY[*]

Water Temperature Fahrenheit	Water high and murky	Water normal	Water low
48° or below	#2	#4	#6
55°	#4	#6	#8
60° or above	#6	#8	#10

At any water level the murkier the water the larger the size of the fly. Basic size for average grease line fishing #6, for deep sunk fly, #4.

[*] Adapted from: *The Art of Salmon Fishing* by Ian Calcott.

Use a deep sunk fly with temperatures below 48 degrees; above this try both greased line and deep sunk methods.

Steelhead Fly Patterns

ROYAL COACHMAN BUCKTAIL

#2/0 - #12   (wet)

Tail: Red hackle fibres
Butt: Peacock herl
Body: Red floss, fairly thin
Shoulder: Peacock herl
Hackle: Natural Dark Brown or Chestnut, tied wet
Wing: White gimp tail*, extending a little beyond bend of hook.

BRAD'S BRAT

Hooks: 4 through 2/0
Tail and tip: Gold for tip; orange and white gimp for tail
Body: Rear half, orange wool; front half, red wool
Rib: Gold tinsel
Hackle: Brown
Wings: One-third orange and two-thirds white gimp tail* white on top
Shoulder: Jungle cock eyes (optional).
   Originated by Enos Bradner, Seattle outdoor writer.

SKUNK

Tail: Scarlet hackle wisps
Body: Black chenille
Rib: Medium oval or flat silver tinsel
Hackle: Black hen hackle beard
Wing: Sparse white gimp tail* or polar bear hair

---

*Gimp tail: Unborn calftail, can be obtained at most fly tying stores. A better substitute for bucktail. The crinkly type is best.

KENNEDY SPECIAL

Tail: Scarlet wisps
Body: Yellow wool yarn
Hackle: Palmered golden badger
Wing: White gimp tail*, sparse
Originated by Mike Kennedy, Oswego, Ore., Kennedy favorite
has same dressing with fluorescent red yarn body.

QUINALT

Tail: Scarlet hackle wisps
Body: Yellow chenille
Hackle: Medium brown
Wing: Cock-Y-Bondhu
Spencer Biddle's favorite

GOLDEN DEMON BUCKTAIL

Hooks: 8 through 2
Tail: Golden pheasant crest feather
Body: Flat gold tinsel ribbed with fine oval gold tinsel
Hackle: Hot orange saddle tied as throat
Wing: Brown grizzly bear hair or red squirrel tail hair
Cheek: Jungle cock
             Original dressing from New Zealand.

Nymphs

Large nymphs tied on #6 and #8-4x long hooks, dark and
light stonefly nymphs most commonly used. This depends on
the prevailing nymphs in the particular stream.

CHAPTER SEVENTEEN

A Steelhead Trip

TODAY IS A BEAUTIFUL warm early June day. We are going to fish together on a small river near Portland, Oregon. This river has both types of steelhead, those produced by natural and artificial spawning. Unfortunately most of the run is derived from stocked fish. There is a hatchery on one of the main branches and the mature fish simply rush right up and swim directly into the hatchery. About three days ago there was a moderate rain. Last night a fly fisherman who lives on the river called me and said the rain had brought a fresh run of fish into the river.

We have reached the river and have set up our rods. Both of our rods have wet tip sinking lines. The water temperature is about 55 degrees Fahrenheit, consequently we will use #6 flies. I will use a Kennedy Special and you a Golden Demon. Both flies are attractors with white gimp tail wings. Bright day, bright fly. However, if we are sure we are fishing over steelhead and do not raise any fish, then we will change to a dull pattern—either a larger or smaller size.

The first pool we will fish is the cut-bank pool, Chapter 9, page 89, Plate 4. Please read this chapter again. In this chapter we used two methods of fishing a fly, first the quartering downstream method of fly presentation, and secondly, the curved upstream cast. The first technique was the "Chuck and Chance It Technique" and the second was the typical "Greased Line Method." Thus these two techniques have been utilized while fishing the same area in the pool. This mixing up of techniques has been popularized in Oregon by two fishing partners, Mike Kennedy and Bill Dame. Their contention is: at one moment steelhead may take a fly with a drag or twitching action, hence the quartering downstream cast, and the next moment prefer a fly with the natural drift of the greased line technique. Consequently, by varying techniques while actually fishing a given area of a stream, you markedly increase your chances of hooking a fish.

Let us assume you have worked the pool thoroughly, using the combined techniques. We know there are fish in this pool, we can see them in the drawing! Remember that steelhead lie and travel at different depths depending upon the temperature and depth of the water. Consequently either add a split shot to the head of your fly or change to a weighted fly. Now go back and fish the pool exactly the same way you did before, and your fly will present itself at a deeper level.

The last time you made one mistake, you did not walk down far enough before you started fishing. Each time move down one-third of your maximum cast. Your longest cast last time was seventy feet, hence move down at least twenty feet before starting over. In this manner you can thoroughly cover just as much water as you did when you only moved down six feet.

Again let me remind you. First use a quartering downstream cast and before moving downstream go over the water again with the quartering upstream method. The faster the water the bigger the mends you must use to keep that fly drifting naturally. This technique will make your fly travel deeper than any other method. One factor you may not realize with this method is no matter the depth your fly travels you will not feel the fish strike, the fish actually hook themselves.

Now that you have fished this pool thoroughly let us walk down the river and look over the next half mile Plates 15 and 16.

The first area we come to is a typical "feeding riffle;" it is relatively shallow but full of rocks. Plate 15. This riffle is fished exactly the same way as the cut-bank hole. However, you will notice an angler standing in the upper part of the picture. He has a problem. He knows there is a steelhead in the vicinity of the rock directly across from him. Because of the terrain he cannot move upstream any farther. There is only one way he can fish that rock. He must cast about six feet above it and then, because of the rapid current in the center, he must put a huge mend in the line an instant after his fly strikes the water. You will notice another even larger rock in the bottom

Plate 15. Feeding Riffle.

of the picture. This time he will be able to wade out above the rock and use a quartering downstream cast but again he must use a large mend to make the fly drift by the rock properly.

The feeding riffle runs into a deep "holding pool," Plate 16. The head of the pool has a very short rapids which goes quickly into deep water. The tail of the pool gradually shallows into the lip and break, Plate 17. The head of the pool is not shown in the two photographs. The photographs reveal that the pool is about one hundred and fifty feet across. The angler shown has gradually worked his way out about one-third the way across; it is obvious that the end of the pool is both shallow and wide. As he waded out he fished his fly just inside the actual break and lip. In the picture he is drifting his fly close to the opposite shore. Then as it approaches the break he will put a mend in his line, and fish his fly across the break with little jerks until

Plate 16. Middle and lower end of holding pool. Fisherman is standing in lower third of pool.

it is directly below him. He will let it hang for a few minutes before he brings it in. He can also turn around and refish the water he covered on his way out. The water just before the lip and break is quite shallow; at times in the summer at dusk it is possible to see steelhead holding in this location. Prince Helfrich, the dean of Oregon fishing guides, emphasizes to his fishermen, "Make the fly swing over the steelhead." Let us suppose there is a fish lying about six feet from the lip just to the left of the fisherman. He should cast downstream so that his fly lands about eight feet directly to the left side of the fish. Then the current will swing the fly across in front of the fish. Wham— a fish is on! The lucky angler will have to scramble downstream to the next pool to land his fish. The technique of allowing a fly to swing across a fish lying in front of the lip of a pool is the secret of the Rogue River guide's success in obtaining steel-

Plate 17. The end of the holding pool, where it gradually shallows into the lip and break.

head for his "dudes." He simply tells his passenger how much line to strip out of the back of the boat. Then he maneuvers the end of the boat so that the fly sweeps back and forth across the lip and break of the pool. When an angler wades and catches a fish he knows his efforts are responsible for the strike.

Below the holding pool is a long shallow reach full of large rocks. Plate 18. Here the river gradually curves to the left over the next mile. This stretch is typical "passage water." We will not spend much time fishing it. The man in the right hand corner of the photograph is simply looking the water over and not fishing. There are numerous large rocks scattered about this section of the river. Around these rocks steelhead often rest while traveling to the holding pool.

A holding pool during high water may become a feeding

Plate 18. Just above the angler standing at right is the same lip and break shown in Plates 16-17. Below him is typical shallow, rocky passage water.

riffle or passage water during low water. Expressed in another way, there are low- and high-water holding pools, feeding riffles and passage water.

From where the angler is standing in the right corner, out in the middle there are rocks. The third rock down usually has a fish near it. Now go down to where the man is standing and carefully wade directly out into the water until you are almost above the rock. Then cast directly to the left of the rock and allow your fly to swing across and in front of it. If this does not result in a strike, walk quietly down the bank until you are about twelve feet above the rock but still standing on the shore and drift a fly by the rock using the quartering upstream technique with big mends in the line. We will walk down this area of the river and fish around a few more rocks.

Our steelhead trip is over; you have been exposed to a great deal of fishing lore. However, I have never met a steelhead who ever read any of the pat rules and theories I mention in this book. The temperature and conditions may be ideal for a fly fished on the surface, yet the fish may only take one close to the bottom. This is what makes this sport so fascinating.

Do not become discouraged because you do not catch fish on each trip. If a fly fisherman catches a steelhead 50 percent of the time he spends on the stream he is an expert. This is a sport for the dedicated, patient man.

Fishing books are a tremendous help, but most learn by being shown. When you meet a fellow fly-fisherman, stop and chat. If you find an experienced one pump him. Experts like to pass on their knowledge to interested novices.

CHAPTER EIGHTEEN

Cutthroat Trout

CUTTHROAT ARE BOTH the easiest and the hardest to catch of all the Pacific Northwest anadromous fish. They detest sunlight. A steelhead will take a fly on a bright cloudless day just as readily as his cousin, the rainbow; a cutthroat seldom. The opportune time is just as the sun is rising or setting, when it is about dark. The best months are from the middle of July to the middle of September. If possible wait for a gentle rain lasting two or three days. The second day is the time to go fishing. However, if the rivers rise appreciably the fish may not bite. When conditions are right they are easy to catch. How many times on a bright clear day have I beaten the water to a froth with nary a fish. On such days the angler will swear there are no fish in the river. Then at late dusk they will materialize from nowhere and for a few short minutes fishing will be good. Cutthroat usually travel in schools, hence it may be an all or nothing situation.

Today we are going to fish one of the Oregon coast streams. We will go down this river in a boat commonly referred to as a McKenzie River drift boat.

This boat was originally developed for the white water of the McKenzie River and is used on all of the rivers of the Pacific Northwest. Actually the river at this time of year is slow and meandering. There are numerous gentle rapids and riffles. In winter months during high water it becomes a river with rapids that require some skill to navigate.

Cutthroat spend the first year of their lives in fresh water. Thereafter they spend about six months in salt water and six months in fresh water. They seldom venture into the main ocean, but are usually found in the mouths of estuaries or bays. Migration down the river occurs in March and April, and they start returning in July. The peak of their runs occur in Septem-

Plate 19. Guide Innes Nestle rowing boat with the late Roy Brunig and his son Bob, on the McKenzie.

ber just before the fall salmon runs. They are often referred to as harvest trout because they appear in rivers at the time of the harvest. After the salmon come, fly fishing for cutthroats usually falls off. They frequently lie below the spawning redds and pick up the occasional eggs that drift out as the female salmon lay them. Cutthroat seldom grow larger than three pounds and a five-pounder is a monster. Most range from twelve to eighteen inches in length. They lack the fighting stamina of their cousins the rainbow. Their usual fight is furious for five minutes with many leaps and then they suddenly quit. As a table fish they are even more delicious to eat than the rainbow. The cutthroat is named for the red slashes on its throat. These are barely visible when they first migrate from the sea, but as they reach the spawning period in January and February they become very pronounced.

Today is a lovely early September day, the rain has been falling quietly for the past two days and conditions are ideal. We are both going to wear waders and rain parkas and as usual our inflatable fishing vests. The weather is warm, the river low and easy to run; at times we will have to drag the boat over some gravel bars.

This river flows part of the time through the coastal fir forests and at other times through meadows. The main industry in this area is dairy farming and cheese production, so beware of the bulls. It is a lovely river, but you will see what an ugly careless animal man can be. The farmers anchor old car bodies against the banks to prevent erosion. Depending on their whims the banks may also be used as trash and garbage dumps.

We will take turns rowing. You stand in the stern, brace your knees against those two projections that jut back into the stern; they are designed for that purpose. A drift boat is usually rowed so the oarsman faces downstream and can read the water in front of him.

Cutthroat may be found in exactly the same places as steelhead but they prefer the tail end of pools and riffles. As a rule they do not like to hold in very fast water, hence the fast upper end of big riffles usually is barren.

We are now coming to a cut-bank pool, Plate 4. Cast quartering downstream as indicated in Fig. 20. There, you hooked one and he was kind enough to be where I expected him to be, that last fish just beyond K in the drawing.

Now we are in a long straight reach with a rather slow current. Against the far shore is a collection of old branches; there is a definite current around them. Cutthroat just love this type of obstruction. Cast in front, by the side, and behind the branches. One rose to your fly just behind the clump but you struck too soon. Try it again — too bad, I guess the boat spooked it. We will run the boat down about one hundred yards, wait a period of time to rest the water and then walk back and fish the spot again. Without the boat to scare them, we should be able to make them rise again.

Cutthroat trout fishing is fun, but it never has been as popular as fishing for rainbows and brown trout. This probably is because they are such elusive fish.

CHAPTER NINETEEN

Silver Salmon

T HE SILVER OR COHO salmon is a magnificent salt-water fly fish. It is rarely taken on a fly in the fresh-water streams of the United States. There are certain streams in Canada where they will take a fly readily. Such rivers are found in the Queen Charlotte Islands off the coast of Western Canada. These streams have one factor in common, they are tidal rivers. When the tide is coming in the flow of the river is reversed and it appears to be flowing uphill. All the flotsam and jetsam drifts rapidly back up the river, much to the confusion of the observer. At high tide the river crests and for a matter of five or ten minutes there is no current. Then the river reverses and flows toward the ocean. At ebb tide the river is at a low point about twenty feet down from its banks. Page 166 Plate 20.

In late September and early October each time the tide changes from ebb and starts back into the river, a wave of fresh Coho salmon sweep up the river. As they come in they jump and boil all over. It is possible to follow the run up the river by the commotion. They usually take a fly when the river is flowing toward the ocean. The best fishing is about one hour before low tide.

Silver salmon prefer a fly cast quartering downstream. The fly is allowed to drift down ten or twenty feet, then retrieved in a slow deliberate manner without any jerks. Jack Meier, another fine Oregon fly-fisherman, demonstrated this technique to me by catching numerous silvers. Fishing almost next to him using conventional Chuck and Chance It techniques I caught nothing. Jack prefers to strip his line into a stripping basket attached by a belt to his waist. After casting the fly, he tucks the rod butt under his armpit and then slowly and deliberately strips the line back into the basket with both hands. He uses a weight forward high density sinking line for this type of fishing. When all the line is back in the basket the fly is cast in a conventional manner, allowing the line to shoot out of the basket. This technique is used extensively by Seattle fly-fishermen for steelhead and other anadromous fish. It is a very effective but slightly mechanical method of fly fishing.

Fred Locke, fish biologist and director of the Oregon Game Commission Stream Programs, has an explanation for the silver salmon's reluctance to take a fly in the rivers of Oregon. These salmon, like other West Coast salmon, belong in the genus

Plate 20. Tillel River, Queen Charlotte Islands, B.C., at low tide.

Plate 21. Coho Jack salmon and cutthroat trout caught at about the same time from the same river. They are difficult to tell apart when they are both fresh in from the ocean.

Oncorhynchus. All die after spawning. They will feed only for a short time in fresh water. Steelhead, cutthroat and brown trout belong to the genus *Salmo* as does the Atlantic salmon. All of these fish have a counterpart that never goes to sea, but spends its entire life cycle in fresh water. Hence when they do arrive in fresh water they maintain a feeding instinct.

The silver salmon in the tidal flow waters of the Queen Charlotte Islands are constantly exposed to brackish water, and thus maintain some feeding instinct.

Just to make matters more confusing, both silvers and chinook salmon will regularly take fresh eggs drifted close to the bottom long after they have returned to fresh water. Such baffling contradictions make fly-fishing a fascinating hobby.

CHAPTER TWENTY

Jacks or Grilse Fishing

THIS IS NOT A new variety of trout or salmon. It is simply nature's clever way of making sure all the female salmon or trout have had their eggs fertilized after they lay them in the redds. They are small, precociously mature males that return early after only spending a year or two at sea. In the case of steelhead and salmon, their average size is from about twelve to twenty inches or from about one-half to three pounds. All of the non-migratory trout also have Jacks or Grilse. I have seen native Rainbow Jacks no longer than eight inches that when opened had fully mature gonads.

Salmon and steelhead customarily travel in pairs of a male and a female; often one or the other dies as they ascend the river of their birth. If the female does not have a mate she will dig a redd with her tail and lay her eggs anyway. It is at this time that the Grilse swings into action. He acts as a substitute mate. He dashes in and fertilizes the eggs. There are always more of these fish than necessary to take care of the lonely ladies. They are scattered throughout the entire run, but the largest concentration is at the beginning and the end of the run.

Nobody seems to know why these precocious males are called Jacks or Grilse. They are called Jacks on the West Coast and Grilse on the East Coast and in the British Isles. Many experienced fly fishermen claim Jacks will take a fly more readily than their mature counterparts. Consequently they fish for them during the optimum times of these fish runs. They are better jumpers and fighters than their larger peers. Silver salmon and steelhead are excellent jumpers when caught in fresh or salt water. Chinook salmon in salt water jump about twenty percent of the time. Their jumps are not nearly as spectacular as the silver salmon. An average jump is about one foot in the air. However, a fresh Silver in salt water and a fresh steelhead in fresh water often jump three to six feet with ease about eighty percent of the time. Winter steelhead do not jump as well or as often as the fresh run summer variety. However, Grilse of all three species are jumping fools.

There is no difference in the manner of fishing for Jacks and Grilse than for the larger fish. Everything written about fly-fishing for steelhead and silver salmon applies to grilse.

The discussion of Jacks and Grilse brings this book to a close. Fly fishing is an art and a science. The art is the part of the sport that allows one to wander aong the banks of a beautiful stream and enjoy the surroundings. The science is the skill with which we read the water and present the fly. The longer you fish, the more important the art will become.

As this book comes to a close, I feel that I have lost a fine fishing partner. However, some day in the near future we will meet again, I hope, in the pages of book currently in preparation, *The Art & Science of Fly Fishing in Lakes.* Till then, good fishing.

Lenox Dick
4717 N. W. Barnes Road
Portland, Oregon 97210

Index